Renewing Higher Education from Within

A GUIDE FOR CAMPUS CHANGE TEAMS

Walter W. Sikes

Lawrence E. Schlesinger

Charles N. Seashore

RENEWING

HIGHER EDUCATION

FROM WITHIN

Jossey-Bass Publishers
San Francisco • Washington • London • 1974

RENEWING HIGHER EDUCATION FROM WITHIN
A Guide for Campus Change Teams
  by Walter W. Sikes, Lawrence E. Schlesinger, and Charles N. Seashore

Copyright © 1974 by: Jossey-Bass, Inc., Publishers
                     615 Montgomery Street
                     San Francisco, California 94111
                          &
                     Jossey-Bass Limited
                     3 Henrietta Street
                     London WC2E 8LU

Library of Congress Catalogue Card Number LC 74-9113

International Standard Book Number ISBN 0-87589-239-6

Manufactured in the United States of America

JACKET DESIGN BY WILLI BAUM

FIRST EDITION

Code 7429

*The
Jossey-Bass Series
in Higher Education*

Preface

Campuses are continually faced with the necessity to innovate in response to internal needs and external pressures. Change teams provide an attractive mechanism for generating such institutional innovation. Many administrators, faculty members, students, and staff have become interested in team development. These people need information about how to build an effective group. In *Renewing Higher Education from Within,* we share the ideas we have accumulated in working with campus teams; the book contains concepts and skills for anyone wishing to start a team or to improve the performance of a team and the satisfactions of members.

Renewing Higher Education from Within combines ideas about campus change with suggestions about practical approaches to team building. The first half of the book contains concepts about the organizational dynamics of campuses, the process of change, and the experiences of campus change teams. In Chapter One we discuss the origins and outcomes of our campus change team project and how it relates to other similar behavioral science projects. Chapter Two discusses the various pressures, both external and internal, that plague campuses today. Highlighted is some material on the personal frustrations in most institutions that require rectifying. In Chapter Three, factors that inhibit change are discussed. We present various individual and group responses to the problems and conclude that teams can usefully combine the best features of other approaches. Chapter Four then spells out the fundamentals of the action-research team approach. Chapter Five presents detailed case histories of each team involved in our project. The final chapter summarizes our findings.

The second part of *Renewing Higher Education from Within* is a manual of practices for starting a team, diagnosing team functioning, recruiting and motivating members, selecting goals, building a team, working for change, connecting to the organization, using consultants, understanding action-oriented research, and facilitating team development. The introduction to the second part of the book describes the organization of that segment in detail.

We have drawn the material in *Renewing Higher Education from Within* from five years of experience with an NTL Institute project titled Training Teams for Campus Change. It was made possible by support from the National Institute of Mental Health (MH 16131). Teams from eight institutions participated in that program; we served as the director, research director, and principal consultant, respectively, of the project. A number of ideas were also drawn from a related project, the Applied Behavioral Science Alliance at the University of Massachusetts, with which two of us (Sikes and Schlesinger) were involved.

Both these projects were based on a model of teams of faculty, students, and administrators, with the assistance of outside consultants, serving as change agents on the campus. The assumption underlying both projects was that teams using a collaborative action-research strategy could best improve the quality of campus life for themselves and for others. A number of other change strategies can also be employed, as we point out in Chapter Four. We do not contend that our action-research team approach is the method of choice for all conditions; but we have concluded that it can play a unique and useful role in generating creative change on many campuses.

The writing of *Renewing Higher Education from Within* was a genuinely collaborative effort. We feel, in fact, that many of the procedures and processes which we discuss were applied by us in writing the book: our personal, interpersonal, and task needs were dealt with; goals were set; commitments were made and re-sources were accumulated; actions were planned and taken; results were evaluated. The particular strengths of each of us were recognized and utilized both in the project and in the writing. A gross oversimplification, but with some truth, is that Sikes was the organizer, Schlesinger the conceptualizer, and Seashore the developer of practical applications of the ideas. There was a high level of sharing, stimulation, and building on each other's ideas during this entire process.

A number of people deserve and have our gratitude for helping to develop and carry out the campus change team project which is the foundation of the book. Stephen Sunderland and Seashore conceived the original notion of the project and wrote the proposal. John Carter, Jane Moosbruker, and William Dyer helped by serving as consultants at times to specific teams. Charles Hamilton, Edith Seashore, Herbert Shepard, and Orion Worden, along with Sikes, consulted with the Applied Behavioral Science Alliance at the University of Massachusetts. The numerous staff members of NTL Institute Higher Education Laboratories helped for four summers in training team members and in testing concepts. Also, many of the assumptions and techniques of consultants and teams have been developed over the past quarter of a century in various other NTL Institute programs.

A special word needs to be said about the campus teams and the Alliance. Their cooperation with us was without exception wholehearted and heart-warming. Working with them has been enjoyable and a uniquely rich experience for each of us. Unfortunately, too many people have been involved on the various campuses to allow naming all those who participated in establishing, supporting, working on, or working with the teams. We express our gratitude to them all.

One set of team members deserves specific acknowledgement because we relied especially on their insights. In November 1973 we conducted a retrieval conference at which representatives from all participating institutions gathered. The purpose of the meeting was to share the learnings from the various campus change efforts and to draw generalizations from them. This event was exciting because of the quality of the persons attending and their rich experiences. The participants also assumed major responsibility for writing the brief team histories in Chapter Five. The participants were: Antioch College, Washington/Baltimore campus: Paul Shoffeitt; State University College at Buffalo: Lebanon Arrington and Richard Meisler; University of California, Davis: Lynn Bailiff and Lynn Marchand; Lesley College: Margaret Buso and James Slattery; the University of Massachusetts: Frederick Finch; the University of Puerto Rico: Luz Beytagh, Celia Cintron, Frances Diaz, and Irma Rodriguez; College of the Virgin Islands: William Delone, Katherine Howard, and W. F. Thomas; the University of Utah: Virginia Frobes and Harris Vincent.

Susan Schwab, Helen Coker, and Karen Ellis each served a stint as secretary to the project. They were invaluable in helping to manage relationships with the teams, accumulate and analyze data, and prepare various drafts of the book. We appreciate their wit, their spirit, and their skill.

Yellow Springs, Ohio   WALTER W. SIKES
Chevy Chase, Maryland   LAWRENCE E. SCHLESINGER
Washington, D.C.   CHARLES N. SEASHORE
September 1974

Contents

Preface   ix

ONE: CONCEPTUAL BASES FOR
CHANGE TEAMS   1

1. Team Origins and Outcomes   3

2. Need for Change   18

3. Blocks to Change and Responses   38

4. The Action-Research Team Approach   53

5. Case Histories of Teams   64

6. Putting It All Together   95

TWO: MANUAL FOR CHANGE TEAMS   109

I. How Teams Get Started   112

II.   Recruiting and Motivating Members   116

III. Selecting Change Goals   121

IV.   Building a Team   129

V.   Working for Change   138

VI.   Connecting to the Organization   144

VII. Using Consultants and Substitutes   148

VIII. Action-Oriented Research   159

IX.   Designs for Facilitating
         Team Development   167

      Bibliography   173

      Index   181

Renewing
Higher Education
from Within

A GUIDE FOR
CAMPUS CHANGE TEAMS

PART I

CONCEPTUAL BASES FOR CHANGE TEAMS

Colleges and universities are struggling with a mind-boggling array of problems which demand innovative solutions. Techniques are badly needed for generating creative changes to meet external demands, institutional requirements, and campus dwellers' personal needs. Teams are a practical mechanism for producing changes which are fruitful for the organizations and the people in them. Such teams join the motivation and personal rewards of sensitivity training groups with the social change which can result from an orientation to task achievement. These teams have several common characteristics: They use some form of calculated data collection and analysis for diagnosis and planning. They consciously examine their own functioning. They basically are collaborative in their change strategies. They try to implement change rather than merely making recommendations to others. They may be initiated by persons with low power in the system as well as by those in official power positions. What team members learn and the relationships they build are viewed as important and valuable outcomes.

The six chapters in Part One give the conceptual bases for

1

change teams. The conceptual model is one of action-research carried out by student-faculty groups with the assistance of outside consultation. This model assumes that there is a felt need for change, that systematic collection of data can provide for an accurate diagnosis of the specific causes of dissatisfaction and for the setting of goals for improvement, and that effective group action can be devised to move toward these goals. Innovation and change are generated by the interplay of research and action.

The material in Part One is drawn from our five-year action-research project with change teams on eight campuses. During this time we tried to facilitate the development of these groups as well as to extend our knowledge about the capabilities which such groups need in order to succeed. The groups were located on campuses of varying sizes, locations, traditions, and styles. The teams worked on curricular reform, grading, racism, sexism, student participation in decision-making, improvement of student services, improvement of teaching, organizational improvement, alternative counseling services, institutional self-study, and professional development.

Our effort to develop, to extend, and to test the conceptual model of change derived from the desire of NTL Institute to apply social science skill and knowledge to educational problems. NTL Institute has been engaged for over twenty-five years in applied behavioral science consulting, research, and training in a variety of settings including businesses, schools, government agencies, hospitals, communities, and colleges. The competencies built during that period have been most useful in our project, the results of which we now report.

1

Team Origins and Outcomes

The origins of this book stem from 1967, when enrollments were booming and campus tensions were building. "Student power" had become a common slogan; educators, editors, and politicians were anguishing publicly about student activism; and campus confrontations were growing in number and severity. In response to these issues, the National Student Association that year conducted a project on reduction of student stress. Stephen Sunderland was a member of the board for that project. The following year he joined the NTL Institute staff and prepared with Charles Seashore a proposal to the National Institute of Mental Health (NIMH) for developing and studying action-research change teams of students, faculty, and administrators on six campuses. The amount granted by NIMH was about one-quarter of the proposed budget, so considerable modification was necessary. Most significantly, paid project directors and research directors on each campus were eliminated; funds for central project staff were substantially reduced, and monies dropped which would have made possible large-scale data collection and analysis. This limitation of funds may well have

3

been serendipitous, in that the NTL staff was required to design procedures for team support and documentation of their efforts which were effective but inexpensive and which developed the autonomy of the campus teams. Thus the experiences of the teams may be more transferable to other campuses than if a more costly model had been built.

Six teams got underway in the spring of 1970. Between then and 1974, a total of eight institutions participated in the project, with none participating for less than two years and three involved for all five years: Antioch College—Washington/Baltimore campus, the University of California at Davis, the College of the Virgin Islands, Lesley College, State University College at Buffalo, the University of Puerto Rico, and the University of Utah. The University of Massachusetts participated during the last two years under substantially different circumstances from the others: it provided substantial support to an interdepartmental group of faculty which wanted to increase its behavioral science skill and knowledge and which wanted to initiate, to support, and to learn from change projects. This group, named the Applied Behavioral Science Alliance, obtained funds for one faculty position which were used to hire four part-time off-campus consultants as it evolved into a network of some seventy people and twenty projects.

The overall goal for the project was to push toward the improvement of higher education. Our immediate objectives were more modest: to support some worthwhile changes, to help team members to have learning experiences, and to learn ourselves. We sought to document outcomes in six areas: (1) learnings of individual team members, (2) team development and functioning, (3) the team's relation to the institution, (4) the team's relation to the change target group or groups, (5) substantive change achieved in institutional programs or processes, and (6) increased use of planned change methods by other groups. We provided consultation to the teams to help them to achieve positive outcomes in these areas.

Each team selected its own change goals. We did not dictate what the goals should be, although we selected teams for inclusion in the project partly on the basis of their interest in working either to improve climate on a campus for teaching and learning, to develop better decision-making processes (including effective involvement of students), or to upgrade the quality of services received by students.

The projects on which the teams worked varied considerably, in spite of these areas of common interest. Teams dealt with changing a university grading system, launching an institutional self-study project, creating a community mental health training program, involving students in institutional decision-making, establishing a peer counseling service, combating racism and sexism, counseling about drug abuse, improving student services, promoting departmental reforms, altering curricula, improving teaching, and upgrading the quality of life in residence halls.

Except for the University of Massachusetts Alliance, teams usually consisted of ten to fifteen members and had one to three projects underway at a time. Often teams went to an NTL Institute training laboratory for two weeks during the summers. Teams received eight days of on-campus consulting and participated in two off-campus workshops each year. The research director visited each campus approximately twice a year to collect data and to share it with teams. Some consulting also was conducted by telephone and correspondence.

During campus visits, project staff identified problems and consulted with the teams. They collected and fed back data from observations, questionnaires, and formal interviews with team members. They conducted interviews with institutional persons outside the group and, where appropriate, shared that information with the team. Consultants also assisted teams with designing questionnaires, training interviewers, designing workshops, designing data collection and analysis procedures, and planning action strategies. The off-campus workshops for teams included laboratory learning processes (in which participants' experiences, interactions, and reactions were the principal component) together with seminars about change theories and methods.

The role of the researcher-documentarian is worth noting. We did not follow the usual model of separating a consulting-training staff, which plans and executes the intervention, from a research staff, which collects and analyzes data for evaluating outcomes. Compared to a typical research model, our approach was more qualitative; it involved more informal interaction between researcher, consultants, and client groups. Consultation activities also included encouraging the team to document its own processes.

The teams differed from each other in many respects but had common characteristics: (1) they were all basically volunteer groups, although occasionally some staff time was paid for by the institution; (2) they employed some variation of a data-based, collaborative strategy; (3) they spent much time in examining their own processes; (4) all teams were significantly involved in selecting their own change goals and projects; (5) each received limited support in workshops and consultation; (6) information was gathered and fed back about the groups' experiences, the capabilities they needed, the things that facilitated their growth, and the things that blocked their effectiveness.

Each year, we collected information from the teams by observation, interview, and questionnaire. These data were used to develop generalizations about the team process, to diagnose team characteristics as a basis for consultation and training, to feed back to the teams to help them in action planning, and to help us in learning to identify significant variables. Models of team development—such as the Group Diagnosis Matrix, Goal Selection Matrix, and the model for assessing team development—were developed and provided to the teams to organize and synthesize information. (All of them are in Part Two of this book.) Teams were asked to identify and to plot significant experiences in the appropriate cells in the Group Diagnosis Matrix, which we devised to enable them and us to see their history in an orderly way; this process also helped teams to get different perspectives on their progress. For example, one team found that all their significant experiences took place *within* the team, which made them realize their neglect in building relationships with other parts of the institution.

Consultant-researcher teams from outside the system have been utilized often in social change projects. Sashkin and others (1973) point out that the most usual pattern is for the researcher to use objective procedures to study the consultant and the system. Benedict and others describe the usual role separation of consultants and researchers: "The diagnostic-training staff which planned and executed the intervention is kept separate from the research staff which develops and analyzes the instruments to measure change. Controls [are instituted] for biases resulting from personal involvement on the part of the change staff and guards against feedback of results which might have contaminated the intervention procedures" (1967, p. 348). In our study, the consultants and the researcher had a division of labor but interacted continuously to assess the state of the teams and the impact of the consultations. These interactions resulted in modifications in the consulting and the development of generalizations about team processes as the project moved along. Hunches and conclusions also were shared and tested with team members during consultating visits and workshops.

The outside consultant-research team gathered data by formal interviews and questionnaires as well as by informal observation and note-taking, information which was shared with the team. This participant-observer method allowed for direct experience and observation while the processes were under way.

Participant-observers who were team members shared with us the task of analyzing the objective social world in which they lived and in the interpretation of their subjective experiences. Our experience parallels that of Bruyn who describes his attempt to make sense out of a change project to the group being studied: "In a field study of how people took action to change local social conditions they deemed undesirable, . . . the observer had to enter into the process itself and interpret it as it appeared to the people engaged. At some points the worker and the subject had to work in concert to obtain an adequate explanation, formulating appropriate descriptive terms and phrasings to explain the change dynamically and personally as it was felt by the people in terms which had meaning for them as well as for the observer" (1966, p. 70). What Bruyn sees as an extension of the participant-observer role, we see as a working principle: the merging of roles in a developmental action-research project which draws on concepts of social system analysis but is closely related to observations and experiential data.

The methodological characteristics which Fairweather (1967) describes as general attributes of socially innovative experiments are similar to this study in these respects: We described and attempted to summarize the empirical evidence about a significant social problem; namely, that many campus inhabitants do not feel the organization is responsive to their goals, energies, and capabilities. We reviewed alternative approaches to social change and provided the rationale for developing project teams to meet individual and campus needs.

The finale of our study was a retrieval conference in which representatives from each project attempted to interpret their experiences and to communicate them to other team members. The consultants and the researcher shared in this process. This step was followed by joint listing of generalizations from members and consultants' experiences. The conferees discussed: team accomplishments, things which happened which the team felt good about and those which it felt bad about, a chronological summary of the significant events in the history of each group, key internal blocks to achievement, key external blocks to achievement, key internal supports for achievement, and key external supports for achievement. The participants brought and used minutes, memos, and research data.

Our study was far short of an experiment in which project teams were compared systematically to other modes of accomplishing the same ends. Experiences in the project teams were, however, compared with the standard procedures for developing innovations in institutions of higher learning; these include decisions made by the chain of command and a variety of group efforts (such as ad hoc committees, standing committees, task forces, work groups, and departmental groups).

The study also was not an experimental evaluation in which observations of the processes and outcomes of innovative and existing social practices are compared. Our efforts were aimed at combining what Bruyn (1966) has called "polar orientations in research"; but we leaned to the subjective mode. We were more interested in understanding social change from the participants' point of view than in seeing events in terms of a formal system. In our analysis we took the chance of overgeneralization rather than risk failing to see the whole context by focusing on data collection and analysis of selected variables. Finally, we tried to see the events as caused by both human purposes and conditions on the campus and in the environment as a whole. In general, we have tried to follow the advice given by Weiss and Rein (1970) in which they make a plea for alternative models which are more qualitative, involve more informal interaction of evaluators with the target group, use observations and documents, and take account of political processes.

Processes and Outcomes

Was the project a success? As compared to the usual bureaucratic methods of introducing innovations, we feel certain that it was but the teams varied considerably in their impact, as the following examples will illustrate.

One of the less successful teams lasted for only two years but during that time it accomplished a number of changes, including a successful generation of pressure for curricular reform—a success which contributed to the team's eventual downfall. One of the team's major sources of frustration was what it perceived as a stodgy liberal arts faculty in an otherwise progressive teacher's college. A liberal arts curriculum study group published a report that recommended changes the team wanted but it met with stiff faculty opposition. The team had the full report published in the student newspaper and distributed clippings of the article to each student. It held an all-student meeting to discuss the report. Its major tactic was organizing a student write-in to faculty expressing strong support for the proposal, which resulted both in faculty voting overwhelmingly in favor of the reform and in a great deal of anger being expressed toward the team for the use of "pressure tactics."

Members of the team were then caught in a conflict between their desires to improve the liberal arts curriculum and faculty and their desires for faculty approval. Several factors made the team avoid further faculty confrontation. After the showdown, they had not generated sufficient internal support to bolster them against faculty opposition. (In a small school, where contact with faculty members is frequent and informal, students tend to wilt in the face of faculty wrath.) Finally, the only nonstudent member of the team was the chairman, an administrative-faculty member; thus the team was seen by some faculty as a missile launched against them by the administration. Evidently student support was not experienced as a sufficient reward in its showdown against an entrenched faculty; in a sense, the success of the team led to its demise.

On the other end of the spectrum, a team in the psychology department of a large university wanted to produce graduates who could perform useful human service jobs as well as go on to graduate school. In its first public confrontation with the faculty, the team was whipped by rebukes from several professors; however, the team had first met with members of the clinical psychology committee, which already favored a more practical psychology curriculum. Moreover, the team had already generated strong student support and had linked up with a faction of the psychology department that supported their views. For external support, a grant received from the dean of social studies was used to survey the need for psychologists in human services and for evaluation of the present program; these survey data provided additional support. Finally, the group had generated strong internal ties: they were able to consolidate their forces, view the faculty's negative reaction as a learning experience, and change their tactics. A variety of ways of disseminating their research report were then used. After the team evicted the head of the psychology department from membership in the team—a move which was widely supported by faculty and students—its power increased dramatically. The change process caught impetus and is now institutionalized in the department. Moreover, team members are translating their new experiences into efforts to change other departments on the campus.

The outcomes on one state university campus illustrate another dynamic. Here, the faculty senate, with administrative urging, had voted to institutionalize student inputs in faculty decision-making in every department. Despite this policy, many departments were noticeably laggard in involving students. A team that was formed around this issue sparred for two years without much success. Its most notable achievement was a doctoral dissertation on attitudes towards student involvement in academic decision-making; although technically adequate, it was of little practical value in steering team action. After two years of desultory activity, the team reached a low point because obviously the faculty gave little support to the cause. In fact, faculty on the team were threatened in their own search for tenure and promotion by being members of the team. There also was little support for student involvement in decision-making from the general student body; for the most part, students tended to be conservative, commuters, individualistic, and career minded. At that point, the administrator who had initiated the team arranged for the creation of several paid positions with part of their responsibilities being improvement of student involvement in decision-making. As members, the job holders became a highly effective core for the team. Student government, always supportive, was even more thoroughly integrated into the team's functioning and provided significant financial support. As a result institutionalization of student involvement in faculty decision-making has been achieved on this campus through the zeal of one administrator, the support of others, a sympathetic student government which was willing to act, and effective team members who had time to work. As a footnote to this team success story, we might note that some team members found that their efforts had a bitter aftertaste, because they were working on goals set by others. As one of them put it, "Don't buy a ticket on somebody else's trip."

The impact of another team was unusual in a different way. We had met with a number of teams successively in a developing college. Its institutional system was underdeveloped, whereas those of all other campuses in the project may be described as over-developed. In fact, we thought what they needed was an agent of stability rather than a change team. The first team we worked with reflected the general characteristics of the school. Students had come to the college primarily because it was perceived as a place where you could "do your own thing." Unfortunately, this individualistic motivation led to little sustained, organized effort, an ethos characterizing the team during the first year. Although members did manage to stay together, a feat which many felt gratified about, they achieved little. The second team we worked with had a goal to achieve accreditation, which might be seen as a drive toward stability. The team was the most organized effort on the entire campus and was highly supported by students and staff. Their goal was virtually unopposed.

In the college's tradition, the team placed a high premium on creativity. At the same time, their organization was primitive.

The team was centered around one faculty member who gave the assignments to team members and to whom they reported about their progress. He also was able to pay for some work. Team plans for ways of presenting the school to the accreditation committee were ingenious, using a variety of media, in addition to the written report, and on-the-scene observation. The key faculty member, however, moved to another position and the team virtually dissolved. It was not able to prepare a final report, and a professional writer was hired for that task.

Now we come to the serendipity aspect of this tale. The change team project has faded from this campus leaving, as far as we know, no meaningful residue except in the learnings of individuals. However, the accreditation process has been altered following the example of this college. Guidelines of the North Central Association now provide for student participation and allow for a wider variety of media to be used in presenting a school to the committee.

The path to institutionalization was far different in another school, a medium-sized state college. The path has some intriguing turns: it begins with a low-power newcomer who was testing his leadership skills and proceeds to the development of workshops to improve communications among top level school administrators. The project was initiated by a student-oriented and charismatic faculty member who gathered into a cohesive group a number of faculty and students who were attracted to him personally. The team developed and funded a call-in, drop-in counseling center run by students. The center continued for fifteen months, but it then foundered because the team did not wish to manage it continuously. The initiator of the team wished to become less central; this produced a time of painful transition during which the chief function of the team was to provide succor and social support to its members; no one reached for the leadership ring on the team merry-go-round. Noting this lack of direction, the consultants finally urged a leadership structure on the team; and a newly arrived black administrator was pushed by the group into the central role. He moved cautiously, building team membership from among his own circle of associates. Some of these new members were associated with a project aimed at integrating economically poorer (mainly black) students into the school. This move, plus the antiracist and antisexist views of other team members, led to a shift of attention in that direction. Workshops were the primary tool of this team. One headed off and settled a crisis with racial overtones between student government and a black students group. Another workshop was held for top school administrators to improve their communications and decision-making skills. The team also has conducted workshops on sexism, drugs, counselor training, securities, and other human relations issues. It has worked with low-power and with high-power groups, which seems to fit the new leader's style and his position. This approach meets the needs of the campus for an organization that can move quickly and skillfully in a number of directions. The team provides members with an emotional home and a base for action in a highly bureaucratic organization.

One team that failed to make any dent on the campus produced some highly effective members who converted their experiences of failure into success in other projects. This team, on a large university campus, was composed mainly of students and student affairs personnel. Apparently looking for an analogy of David and Goliath, they tried to change the grading system and fell into the trap expressed as buying a ticket on another person's trip. The team took on this task at the urging of a dean of students, who saw the transcript and grading system as a main source of student stress, because of both their attraction to the dean (who had initially formed the project) and their frustration at efforts to find a feasible and interesting project. The team exhibited a high level of planning skill and energy. They gathered data by surveying student attitudes toward grading and by collecting reports on the effects of grading; they studied alternative grading and record-keeping systems; they interviewed deans and experts on grading. But unfortunately, the dean departed before the team got going.

After two years of effort, the team had mobilized practically no faculty support. Only one regular faculty was a member. Nor was it supported by any other significant group on campus. At the same time, the team was highly energetic, enjoyed acquiring skills in group dynamics, and members were fascinated with their learnings about the process of change. Perhaps, except for the team leader, the team was more interested in learning about change than in accomplishing their change goal. The team finally made a concerted effort at influence when a faculty council was to decide on a committee recommendation to change the grading system. It had made considerable contributions to the recommendation and favored the proposed changes. The consultants helped the team to put together an action strategy and to mobilize its energies. Team-members called individually on about two-thirds of the faculty council to discuss the proposed grading changes. They presented all members of the council with an organized report on the effects of grading practices, and they put together a lobbying group of students and staff. The faculty group voted down the proposed changes by a vote of seventeen "for" and twenty-four "against." To see what it could learn from this experience, the team did a follow-up survey. The faculty members indicated that their personal experiences in grading practices had counted far more heavily than did any other factor, including the team's efforts, in their decisions.

The team faded into oblivion, having chosen a target that was beyond its resources and failed to mobilize the endorsement needed to give some weight and credibility to their research utilization effort. On the redeeming side, the team members felt good about their experiences, and several reported subsequent large-scale change projects where the skills they had gained made a critical difference in their success. One lesson to be learned from this history is that the faculty, in deciding against the change, were behaving predictably and sensibly. People seldom change their views on the basis of rationally presented facts: they think and act on the basis of their own experiences. The problem the team did not solve was to devise a strategy for making the facts about grading part of that faculty's life experience.

An interdepartment network of change agents and project teams at another large university has many unusual characteristics that increase its potential for campus improvement. This project became part of the study late in our work; as of this writing, it has had about two years of experience. The project was started independent of our study but was linked to it through common consultants and research support from the grant. Its large, heterogeneous membership gives the network a greater critical mass than that of the other campus teams. Many people with common interests, located in different parts of the campus, are developing a variety of ways of working together effectively. A chief asset is to be able to act as change agents for one another. They have demonstrated, for instance, that a faculty member from the School of Business, who has little clout within his own school, can be very effective at promoting useful change in the School of Nursing. They have also demonstrated that many faculty and students are attracted to the possibility of working on projects while advancing their professional and personal growth. Two dozen projects and a variety of training activities have been sponsored. Unfortunately, after sixteen months of funding the consultants, the administration, because of financial pressure, indicated it possibly would not continue that support. The group's attention then was deflected from developmental and project work to trying to resolve financing, which stunted group development at a crucial point. The network nevertheless has made several indelible changes in the campus and seems destined to make more. It should be noted, too, that administrative support was an initial key to extension of the network beyond a small, nuclear core group.

One of the most controversy-ridden teams was in a small, and isolated, public college. This team was often successful in rearranging campus conditions to be more favorable to students; but it also had many difficulties. First, the dean of students, who initiated the team (and incidentally wrote his doctoral dissertation about it), was evidently perceived by other top level administrators as building a separate power base and pushing in a direction they did not choose. He was eased, not too gently, from his job. This action temporarily stopped the flow of energy into the group. Fortunately for the team, the ex-dean continued to work with it and to provide initiative. It was also important that two faculty members who stayed with the team had excellent reputations with the students and were apparently trusted by the administration. Second, the team was moving into territory traditionally staked out by the student council, which challenged the usurpers; considerable time and energy was spent in reconciling the claim of each group for the "turf." Accommodation was reached when team leaders also became student council leaders. Another major difficulty of the team was its connection to the bureaucratic structure. Although all teams were linked to the chain of command that mandated their existence, on larger campuses, groups tended to drift free of the structure. In this small school, the team's activities are carefully monitored by the power figures to see if they threaten their values and goals—and the administration did try to curtail the group's activities. The team, however, is currently engaged with energy and skill in a major project: starting a radio station. If that effort is successful, it will have a major impact on the campus.

Outcomes for Team Members

Team members have been nearly unanimous in agreeing that the group experience made them more aware of changes needed in the college. They also noted acquisition of knowledge and skills. There is no doubt participants have learned much about their institutions, group processes, and themselves; and in these respects, we think the groups have been very successful and satisfying.

Most members were highly committed to their project team. Frequently, however, there was a gap between feelings of commitment and actual work by members on projects. A large majority indicated a high level of interest and involvement, but only half felt that the time they spent in the group matched their commitment. Nearly half felt guilty about spending too little time in group activities; in contrast, few felt eager to spend too much time in group activities. Another aspect of commitment is the degree of change desired by most team members. Most teams did not attract radicals; members were neither conformists nor rebels but were advocates of reconstruction, reflecting a broadly humanistic commitment oriented to personal growth and development and to improvement of the college. The concerns of team members were intense. Although they had little formal power, a sizable group felt that team membership increased their influence both on campus and in their groups. Although team members thought they had learned a good deal about diagnosing problems and planning for change, they felt much less confident about their capacity to move others on campus to be aware of the problem, to commit themselves, and to work for a solution. In other words, they were unconfident of their ability to move from planning onto the public stage of the campus. The kind of authority most team members preferred, as might be expected, was based on expertise, personal style, and competence—it was not based on age or position. They were also highly motivated to increase their own power by increasing their knowledge and skills. However, they were not sure of their abilities to generate enough force to achieve their goals.

2

Need for Change

The 2,400 or so institutions of higher learning in the United States are processing about half of the college age population. Over nine million students are enrolled in colleges and universities; higher education is big business. Not only is it a major industry (sometimes the biggest in a state), but these institutions and their products—skilled people and knowledge—are viewed by some as the major steering element in our technological society. However, new problems emerge as old forms of education fail to fit new faces, or as support dwindles, or as the influx of new faces slows down.

Partly because of its size and importance, critics are flailing away at the higher education system and are calling for reform and renovation in many areas. At the institutional level, the critics claim, colleges are not sure whether they are monasteries passionately devoted to the pursuit of truth or ministers to ailing communities. Colleges are concerned with both the art of living and the art of making a living. They highlight an essential core liberal arts curriculum and send their inhabitants abroad to deal with culture shock. They emphasize historical knowledge to avoid the mistakes of the past and problem-solving skills to avoid future errors. They house large libraries and nests of T-groups. Alongside

18

the new policies of open admissions, they serve as clearinghouses for the future elite of education, government, and industry. They talk about learning and emphasize credentials. They talk about faculty-student relations and reward research. They stress the integration of learning and are baronies of specialization. The list of dilemmas and paradoxes is long. A core problem is that many of these organizations, understandably, are unclear about their function. They are concerned with fighting for survival in days of dwindling resources, militant faculty organizations, critical students, and hostile legislatures. We sympathize with these problems and, although we claim no magical insights, we think we can offer some helpful ideas.

The human problems generated by institutional uncertainty are numerous. On many campuses the inhabitants feel lonely, isolated, hostile, competitive, insecure, and anxious. They often feel powerless to change "the establishment" or to control their own lives. Institutions, by and large, offer few opportunities for members to shape themselves and their environments. Campuses offer little encouragement for simultaneously learning to comprehend, to feel, and to create; to take risks and to behave autonomously; or to connect with other people who share one's commitments.

Drucker (1973) has offered a prescription for colleges: They are difficult to manage, he claims, because they are not clear about their basic mission. Universities should impose on themselves the discipline practiced by managers of successful service organizations. They should think through carefully the different, often conflicting, alternative functions and then work out an overall mission unique to each institution. From such goals would flow the specification of objectives, selection of priorities, and the basis for measuring performance.

We feel that this perspective is excellent, to the extent that these institutions are hierarchically organized and managed. However, management in higher education seems more closely allied to the art of politics than to running IBM. The administration that seeks to manage strongly is accused of being dictatorial and is told that it is there to serve the faculty. The administration that fails to point the way and to push is accused of lack of leadership. Meanwhile, many changes that do take place on the campus stem from student activists, community pressures, government initiatives, and the interests of foundations. Few successful changes are internally initiated.

To put the matter mildly, there is currently great disagreement about the desired purposes, methods, and styles for institutions of higher learning. Casual reading of the general news magazines reveals a diverse set of opinions ranging from Jacques Barzun's intellectualism, to Max Rafferty's pleas for strong authority, to Ivan Illich's antiestablishmentarianism, to Tom Hayden's cries for campus revolution. Every group seems bent on capturing the campus as a base from which to exercise influence, a strategy that makes some sense because a key function of colleges has been the allocation of persons to influential roles, positions, and careers. Beyond that common purpose of higher education, the shared objectives of institutions are less obvious.

External Factors

Outside events—war, prosperity, depression, sputnik, and the civil rights movement—have powerful consequences on campuses. At the time we started this project, the militant student movement was reaching maturity. Kent State was just around the corner, and the University Without Walls was not off the ground. There was great concern about violence on campus, the war, drugs, ROTC, recruiting blacks, defense research policies, and university real estate practices. None of these issues were solved during the five years of the campus change team project, but the stage and the players changed a great deal; one has to keep moving to keep in touch with emerging issues.

Although such outside influences clearly are major factors in causing or supporting changes on campuses, institutions fail to change, in good measure, because external factors do not require, encourage, or support innovation. In either case, the environment in which colleges or universities exist is an important consideration in looking at their adaptive behaviors. Hefferlin (1969, p. 146) concludes "that while the responsiveness of an institution to change can be significantly affected by internal factors, the institution will seldom alter its functions without external influence. Outsiders initiate; institutions react."

The experiences of Antioch College since 1965 illustrate the magnitude of problems which stem from external forces, in this case the drive for racial integration and government funding.

In 1965 the Rockefeller Foundation gave Antioch College and five other small "elite" institutions, a substantial grant to help in bringing so-called disadvantaged students, primarily racial minorities, to the campus. The college used that money as a base from which to build a more pluralistic community. In 1969 the board of trustees made a commitment to a substantial increase in the number of "New Directions" students. By 1972–1973 these students amounted to 10 percent of the population on the Yellow Springs, Ohio, campus. Most were blacks; all were from socio-economic backgrounds which would not normally have produced students for a selective, middlewestern, private college. All had great financial needs. They were supported by a combination of money from students' earnings, family contributions (often zero), financial aid from the college, loans, state grants, private contributions, and particularly federal funds—which were crucial to the college's ability to maintain this unusual and daring program.

In spring 1973, President Nixon announced that he was impounding the funds from which Antioch was getting the money for New Directions students. This action had been preceded by cues that both the method of distribution of federal aid and the total dollars allocated were in for substantial revision. It was certainly clear that the executive branch, at any rate, had little interest in continuing to support programs such as Antioch's. Both the college administration and the New Directions students were badly shaken by these events. The students demanded guarantees of future support which the college felt it could not make in view of the uncertainties about federal funding. The New Directions students and their supporters struck. The campus was closed for six weeks and was reopened by police action following a court order gained by nonstriking students. At least partly as a result of these events, admissions have fallen drastically, the college faces a deficit of over half a million dollars for 1973–1974.

Important ingredients in creating this situation were the push for racial justice and integration of the mid-sixties, increasing militancy of minorities, the interests of a large foundation, federal policies, shifts in governmental priorities, and power struggles between the President and Congress. There was also psychological support from several quarters for Antioch's efforts to become a pluralistic institution. (For example, the work of the Newman Task Force on Higher Education and the Carnegie Commission encourage movement toward pluralism.)

External support and encouragement (or discouragement) have profound consequences on institutions. Key parts of this support-and-influence system are state and federal agencies, governmental policies, foundations, educational associations and study commissions. Linking to these agencies and organizations can be of great value to a campus team. For instance, many teams have told us that being connected with NTL Institute has been of great help to them in increasing their status and influence. Other teams have acquired grants which have given their work legitimacy and prestige within their institutions.

Many other external factors make up the setting of institutions in the mid-seventies. These are variables with which change efforts must cope and are apparent to most observers of the scene so we will describe them only briefly in the following paragraphs.

The decrease in income of colleges and universities makes it more difficult to add innovative programs. More either/or choices must be made. Hefferlin (1969) points out that in the past most new ventures have not replaced old activities but have been offered in addition to existing programs.

The pool of college age persons is shrinking and the percentage of high school graduates going on to college is declining. In some cases, increased competition for students produces innovations calculated to attract them: 4-1-4, foreign study, contract learning, and experiential opportunities. More typically, institutions seem to eliminate the "frills" as the cash flow slows down—and innovative programs often are perceived as frills.

The prestige of higher education institutions and their leaders has taken a severe battering in recent years. A ground swell of confidence in the system was maintained until the beginning of the 1970s; now it has dropped to a ripple. There is no longer the boundless (and, unfortunately, groundless) optimism that cranking more and more young people through college will provide solutions to our national problems.

Those who aspire to be change agents on campus must capitalize on shifts in values and interests among students and faculty. Currently, the mainstream of university students appears as career or marriage oriented as it was ten years ago, but a substantial segment is seeking new life styles, new ways of learning, new forms of relationships, and more humane criteria for success. For instance, the eldest daughter of one of the authors graduated in 1973 with a degree in education from one of the "highly selective" liberal arts colleges. She and three friends, all with at least four years of college, and all looking for a practical course to downward mobility, spent their first several postcollege months in building a house with their own hands. They are sensible and delightful young people seeking a way of living which is less consumption oriented and less controlled by "the establishment."

Another shift in values and interests is described by Cross (1971) in her discussion of "new students" (those who have not typically been in college and who have different motivational and achievement patterns). They may be older, minority members, or may come from other untraditional backgrounds.

Clearly, another push for change has been governmental insistence that institutions promulgate programs to eliminate discrimination against women and minority group members. Unfortunately, progress is slow. Racism and sexism still abound on campuses. The *Chronicle of Higher Education,* October 9, 1973, reported that in 1970, of college and university fulltime faculty, 22.5 percent were women and 5.3 percent were minorities. The prediction by the Carnegie Commission on Higher Education is that these figures will by 1980 increase only to 28.1 percent and 7.4 percent, respectively. Of course, as rank goes up, the percentages of women and minority faculty drops radically. Only 8 percent of full professors are women.

We recommend the action-research change team approach as a good one to use in dealing with problems of racism and sexism. In working on these issues it is often necessary to gather information, to link various institutional resources together, to promote attitudinal change, and to provide support for persons in uncomfortable positions. These are things which teams can do particularly well.

A relatively new external factor is the presence of unions on a growing number of campuses. The unions both win and lose some elections, but the trend is distinctly in their favor. Meeth (1971, p. 40) concludes, "if administrative officers do not want a faculty union, they have to adjust the traditional forms of college administration." Unless the structures bend or yield great amounts of authority, information and exclusivity, unions will rapidly grow, he says.

Other Pressures

Conflict over purposes of higher education. The Carnegie Commission (1973, p. 1) listed the main purposes of higher education in the United States as:

> The provision of opportunities for the intellectual, aesthetic, ethical, and skill development of individual students, and the provision of campus environments which can constructively assist students in their more general development and growth.
> The advancement of human capability in society at large.
> The enlargement of educational justice for the postsecondary age group.
> The transmission and advancement of learning and wisdom.
> The critical evaluation of society—through individual thought and persuasion—for the sake of society's self-renewal.

That list seems unexceptional but even these items contain seeds of conflict: Why is emotional development of students not included with intellectual, aesthetic, ethical, and skill development? Why, in fact, are students apparently the only persons in a college to develop? Does educational justice mean reparations to minorities for past crippling discriminations? Should institutions of higher education stand as critics of society; and, if so, will the state legisla-

tures continue to support them? The Commission (1973, p. 4) lists
its own questions about other controversial issues about the purposes
of higher education:

>   Should there be a concern for the student *as a
> total* person?
>   Should *special consideration* be given to members
> of minority groups and women?
>   Is there now an *unfair discrimination in favor of
> the college attender?*
>   Should higher education seek to further *equality
> of opportunity* with differentiated results *or a flat equal-
> ity of results?*
>   Should organized faculties . . . *take positions on
> political controversies?*
>   Should the campus become an important base for
> *promoting a new type of society?*

Disagreement over such questions characterizes reactions to
higher education. Agreement about what colleges and universities
are supposed to be doing is very limited and the confidence of the
people that schools are doing it well is even more limited. The
Carnegie Commission is probably wise in listing as the first of its
priorities for action the clarification of purposes. The conflicts derive, however, from differences which exist in society at large and
thus are not totally resolvable within single institutions.

Hefferlin (1969) points to a different kind of goal for educational institutions: *continuous adaptability* which brings change
beyond sporadic and occasional reforms, reacting to crises, and
spurts of housecleaning followed by years of inertia. This "process"
goal has a similar flavor to Taylor's (1969, p. 121) description
of the ideas of the experimental colleges of the 1920s and 1930s.
"We wanted a community in which the talent and individual character of each person who entered it—teacher, student, administrator—would have a full chance to grow in its own terms. We wanted
an open-handed style of life and learning which would grow and
change through the plans made by the members of the community
working together. There would be joy there and a sense of easy
comradeship."

Hodgkinson (1971) points out that there is a disjuncture between what large segments of the American public are demanding and what many college students are saying. The public wants higher education to justify itself in terms of goods and services. Students, on the other hand, more likely say that colleges and universities should end their role as certifiers of people to provide services. A real "catch 22" type of resolution to this dilemma is provided by an advertisement in the winter, 1973–1974 *Change* magazine: "unless you want 'yes' men, don't say 'no' to the college of your choice." This appeal for public support for institutions thus is based on the need to train dissenters who ultimately will be assets to the establishment.

Differences in the visions of individuals about the missions of colleges and universities pose problems for change groups within institutions. It is difficult to attain consensus about a subgoal, such as a project for the team, if overall goals are in dispute. It is also hard to work with a collaborative style in a climate where there is a high level of conflict about broad institutional purposes. We experienced this problem with the University of Puerto Rico when it became completely polarized on the issue of independence. Team members also differed on this issue; it was difficult to establish even a low-level goal because every act was read for its political message. Suspicion was high; gaining energy for nonpolitical activities was difficult. Everyone's views on educational purpose were determined by political values. This team was pleased at being able successfully to confront those differences among its members and move into action, whereas most other campus groups were stalemated.

New methods and programs. In spite of many innovative efforts, the form of higher education today has changed very little from that which prevailed when the authors were in college (or, for that matter, when our parents were in college). A small percentage of faculty and students, however, have made significant improvements in methods of teaching and learning. These innovative programs provide examples and energy for other campus change efforts.

There are now a few nontraditional institutions: Antioch College, Johnston College, Hampshire College, SUNY at Old Westbury, Goddard College, the Evergreen State College, New

College at Sarasota, University of California at Santa Cruz, Thomas Jefferson College, and Livingston College have consciously tried to design their total programs to produce nontraditional teaching and learning experiences. There also are specific innovative programs in many otherwise traditional institutions, for example: the accelerated learning program at Buffalo State College, Orchard Hill at the University of Massachusetts, the human relations program at Queens College, and University Without Walls units on about twenty-five campuses.

The assumptions and methods vary among these programs, as do their successes, but, in general, their values are more humanistic, student centered, and democratic than are traditional programs. The techniques tend to be experiential, individualized, and process oriented as opposed to a focus on content exclusively. Harrison (1969, p. 304) clearly lays out the values which undergird many nontraditional programs and classes:

> We need to convert students from institutionally directed education to self-directed education. We need to move students from reliance on authoritative sources of information toward developing and evaluating their own sources. We need to move from a focus on the content of learning to an equal and sometimes greater concern with the process of learning. That is, we need to be at least as much concerned that the student in our classroom learns how to continue to learn as we are that he learns the facts, principles, and theories we present to him there. We need to change educational systems in which the learner is primarily a passive recipient of learning, by designing systems in which students actively create their own learning. We need to move from a criterion of learning that stops with achievement measured in the classroom toward a focus on application in the real world.

Rogers discusses the characteristics which many innovative teachers and their students are seeking: "Let me define a bit more precisely the elements which are involved in such significant or experiential learning. *It has a quality of personal involvement*—the whole person in both his feeling and cognitive aspects being *in* the learning event. *It is self-initiated. . . . It is pervasive*. It makes a difference in the behavior, the attitudes, perhaps even the personality of the learner. *It is evaluated by the learner*. He knows whether it is meeting his need, whether it leads toward what he *wants* to know, whether it illuminates the dark area of ignorance he is experiencing" (1969, p. 5).

A *group* operating with the values which Rogers emphasizes is a logical method for trying to move learning in the directions to which he points. Groups are very useful in achieving the goals of participation, initiation, and involvement.

Despite the changes and innovations that have already been effected on some campuses to make a compromise with today's world and resolve some problems we have pointed out, there is extensive dissatisfaction with the conditions of living and learning. The dissonance between the facts of life and the ideals of inhabitants give rise to the search for alternatives; the search is buttressed by the expectation that education is intended to help people to shape reality as well as to adjust to it. These feelings can be converted into action *if:* they are shared rather than remaining private; people join together in mutual support, to form a group that develops relationships emphasizing trust, good will, and cooperation; the process of the group leads to a continuous development of new knowledge, increased resources, and increased potentiality for taking action; and the group builds links to other parts of the campus to increase understanding and support. The basic premise of this strategy is that social change can be initiated by individuals with feelings which are articulated and validated in cooperative groups. They can then take action to modify the campus environment.

Personal Frustrations

I get lost in the system. Members of institutions often feel a lack of connection with the forces which are influencing their lives. Dissatisfaction can flow from feelings of getting lost in the system. Students, faculty, and at least low-level administrators make comments such as: "I feel powerless." "I am uninformed about what is happening in the university." "It is difficult to get things done." They do not feel effectively engaged with what goes on in the school of which they are a part; nor do they see themselves as cared about by the institution or as in control of their destiny, for they are unable to represent themselves in decision-making.

This is what a young woman student member of a team from a small experimental college said in an interview with us about order, information, influence, and involvement:

> I don't like a tight ship where you must do this at a certain time every day and if you take a course, you have to have three exams. You can't have any alternative like going up to your teacher and saying, "I can't take an exam too well, I'd like to write a paper, instead. Would that be OK? You can suggest books to me and tell me what kind of thing you'd like but since I'm better at writing papers, I think I should be able to do that. . . ." I went to school before for two years and it was a different type of institution, 40,000 people about. . . . I wasn't particularly involved in anything to do with the way the school worked; I was pretty much just taking my courses and that's why I left—because I didn't enjoy just taking courses and not feeling like I was getting anything out of it. I've learned that I can enjoy doing other things and I feel more capable. . . . I guess (being a member of this team) has increased my confidence somewhat in that I can do different things and that I can enjoy it and produce things and get something done.

Heist interviewed fifteen recognized creative people who had graduated from five different institutions, and all expressed similar reactions to the woman quoted above. He reports: "The most frequent reactions . . . dealt with a described rigidity or inflexibility of the 'system.' In this respect, they spoke critically of colleges as organizations and referred to the trivial regulations and established traditional curricula that seemed to change very little. A majority of men and women spoke of the pressures and constraints on their time and lives . . . a vague pressure experienced and transmitted by instructors and students. . . . To them, college education seemed an enforced detour which kept them from essential perceptual and emotional satisfactions" (1968, pp. 52–53).

Further evidence of students feeling out of touch with the

system is provided by a survey at Stanford University. The *Chronicle of Higher Education* of December 12, 1973, reported that the study showed that students feel that their contacts with faculty members are marked by an ethos of impersonality and low levels of interaction. While about two-thirds of the students are satisfied with the intellectual climate and quality of instruction, only one in three is satisfied with the quality of student-faculty relations and the advising system.

As do other bureaucracies, institutions tend to establish policies and procedures more to meet the needs of the system than to meet the needs of individuals. (This is not to say that these two sets of needs are necessarily opposed.) Dormitory policies usually deal first with needs of the maintenance department, the bursar's office, and the director of housing; residents' needs may then be considered. Grading policies are usually based on the desires of graduate schools, employers, and registrars than on the effects of grades on learning. Tenure and contract renewal processes are more responsive to administrators' desires for control, order, and measurability than on the need to enhance the growth of faculty members. Psychological services derive more from the convenience of the staff and their models of therapy than from a real diagnosis of student and faculty needs. Budget processes are often misapplied industrial models. Consequently, many members of institutions do not feel connected, cared about, or influential. Team membership can help to fulfill those needs.

I do not use and expand my capabilities. Another cluster of dissatisfactions expressed by inhabitants of colleges and universities is being unable to utilize their abilities to serve their own goals or even institutional objectives. Typical comments are: "My activities are irrelevant to me and to the institution." "I have unused resources." "I am more capable than I am allowed to be." "I am not learning what I want to learn."

Many students feel that they are marking time, or killing time, while they wait to get a certificate or grow up so they can go out and "live." They do not see their college experiences, at least the formal parts, as serving either utilitarian or personal growth purposes. A faculty member of a campus team working on changing a psychology program in a large university said in an interview:

"I have been hearing for so many years the students complain that the curriculum doesn't prepare them to go out into life and perform the kind of duties the different jobs require. So I expect by defining some of these problems that we will really influence making the curriculum more vital, more relevant, and provide them with the skills they think they need when they get out of here."

Faculty as well as students often feel their capacities are not fully utilized; they cannot make full contributions; they do not grow and learn from participation in institutional processes. A young faculty member commented on his favorable reaction to involvement in a team which was trying to set up a new counseling service as compared to earlier committee experiences: "I think this project is going to get off the ground and that it will work and be a positive experience for me in that respect. Also, I'm learning a lot. I've never quite had this role in an institution. I've always been a sort of junior partner in this kind of venture. And this is the first time in this sort of thing that I've been a central figure, and there's a lot of learning and growth involved in that. . . . I'm sort of testing out my ability to bring a group of people together and serve as an agent in having them be productive. . . . I've at times been a member of teams like that but always when the person who was a main catalyst for it was somebody else, somebody older, and it's really interesting to try to play that role."

On the other hand, faculty members sometimes feel vulnerable for trying to involve themselves in the development of the institution. In another team, the chairman was a young sociologist. He had been appointed to the team as a part of his faculty responsibility by the vice-president for academic affairs. The goal of the group was to improve student involvement in decision-making. The sociology professor was put under considerable stress by messages, both subtle and direct, from his department chairman and colleagues that he should not become identified as a supporter of student participation or it would go against him in his quest for tenure. Similarly, in working with other campus groups, many faculty told us that they really enjoy being members of improvement teams, that they like to contribute and learn in that way—but they cannot afford to take time away from activities which the institution will reward.

Even vice-presidents of institutions prize opportunities to use their resources on ventures which really intrigue them and which they can enjoy. One, who was a member of the group working on improving student participation in decision-making, reported: "Well, I've enjoyed very much being involved in the group. In the first place, it's something pretty close to my heart. I was glad to be given a chance to do what I wanted to do. I wanted to get on a subcommittee because I guess I had a lot of suggestions about things I felt needed to be done that I could directly intervene in. So I was glad to get in it. I've enjoyed it. I'm very much committed to it and I feel it is one of the most significant things we have on the campus. And I am enjoying working with the people. We do have a good time in addition to the work."

Music critic Ralph Gleason (1968) says the main problem of educating creative people is not a matter of discipline; the main problem is that by the time they reach college age, students are faced with an enormous, rigid structure and organization. This structure also is reflected in the overall attitudes of many of those who maintain the institution, preventing creative people from getting to those experiences most important to them. The system asks creative people to spend much time in activities which are of no interest to them. It is no wonder that students who are identified as creative tend to drop out in higher numbers than do their less creative peers. For instance, Chickering (1971) reports Snyder's finding that students at Massachusetts Institute of Technology who scored high on Omnibus Personality Inventory scales used to identify the creative personality were most likely to leave the university.

Argyris (1957) has observed that basic conflicts exist between the needs for personality development and the requirements of bureaucratic organizations. Colleges and universities are bureaucracies and even though their purpose is to support learning, they may generate the same growth-inhibiting dynamics as do other bureaucracies. Persons working in pyramidal organizations, particularly at lower levels, tend to become dependent, passive, use short time perspectives, and develop only shallow interests. These characteristics are the opposite of those we usually associate with maturity.

Pyramidal values are implicit in the functioning of colleges and universities; one has only to look at typical relations between a teacher and students in a class, the use of grades, decisions on tenure, or how deans and faculty interact to provide examples. Many students, faculty, and staff respond by rebellion, withdrawal, emotional distress, attempt to climb the ladder, and, occasionally, participate in institutional change efforts.

The concept of psychological success of Lewin and others (1944) provides theoretical support for the project teams we are discussing. They said that psychological success requires that organizations provide individuals with opportunities to define their own goals which are related to their central needs, to define their paths to these goals, and to have the achievement of the goals present a challenge. In our observation, many people in colleges and universities do not have those opportunities and experiences.

Feldman and Newcomb, after extensive review of studies on the effects of college, endorse these conclusions about the effects of the pyramidal organization of educational institutions: "The formal, hierarchical organization is an instrument of great effectiveness; it offers great economies over unorganized effort; it achieves great unity and compliance. But its deficiencies include great waste of human potential for innovation and creativity and great psychological cost to the members. . . . The modification of hierarchical organization to meet these criticisms is one of the great needs of human life" (1969, p. 222). This statement leads us to examine a third set of dissatisfactions.

I am unhappy. This emotional state evokes such comments as: "I am lonely." "I am bored." "I feel under great stress." "I am confused." "I am angry." Again let us emphasize that these feelings are by no means universal. Many students and faculty are cheerful, enjoy their relationships, and are happy with what they are doing. On the other hand, there are common institutional processes which may generate negative emotional states and stress. For instance, students usually work on tasks that are created and assigned by someone else; they have little or no voice in choosing goals in courses or in devising ways to meet those goals; they are subject to rules and regulations over which they have little influence. Living and social arrangements provide little support for developing satisfying relationships with others—particularly nonstudents. Grades are experienced as controlling and, often, punitive. In short, conditions on campuses often lead to psychological failure rather than to success.

In an interview with us, a male senior on a team which was trying to change the university's grading system discussed the campus situation and the work of his group:

> It's exciting working on this project, in a sense, because the thing I'm really turned on to is how the learning environment affects an individual's ability to learn and what he learns and how he feels about that. Parts of the environment are the buildings, and other parts are like policies and regulations. All these affect how the individual student responds—how he learns. . . . One of the things that colleges do is tend to limit or weaken the experience the student will have by using grades in a way that creates an artificial force. Then gradually, because of the nature of it, students will come to depend on grades for motivation rather than relying on their natural curiosity which could be developed. . . . Developing curiosity and supporting interest is more difficult than bombarding someone with the need to achieve academically. . . . I think it's much more rewarding when students have the chance to become self-motivated. Twenty to thirty percent of the students [we studied] felt punished, which is a pretty strong term, by knowing there were low grades on their transcripts, and that's a heavy penalty.

Apparently most students do not support the typical letter grading system, which, according to a 1973 survey conducted by the American Council on Education (Creager, 1973), is used in 96.7 percent of colleges and universities. A survey at the university referred to in the above quotation revealed that 83 percent of upperclassmen felt the grading system should be changed. Scores of studies of grading have indicated virtually no relationship between grades and any measure of adult success. Grades have been shown to have adverse effects on learning, to be unreliable, and to be damaging to the development of even honors students. The data are clear and consistent. As Axelrod (1968, p. 121) says, "Course grades have not been found to constitute a reliable index to any dimension—past, present or future—of a student's work or life, except other school grades."

Nevertheless, the faculty senate of the university mentioned above, after reviewing this kind of information, has three times in two years voted down all efforts to improve the A-F grading system. That behavior can be very frustrating and angering for people subject to those decisions. It is particularly galling in institutions which profess to honor research and rationality.

The flavor of the feelings of unhappiness from which many inhabitants of college and universities suffer are nicely expressed in an essay which Paul Spike wrote when he was a senior at Columbia University and is included in Hodgkinson (1971, p. 159):

> What I am really saying is that we have not yet found the answers to personal and social happiness. The hippie experiment, for example, was an attempt to derive such answers from dropping out and establishing new life styles on the fringes of society which would be full of joy and rich with fulfillment. That experiment is just about finished. . . . Student movements in this country, as anyone who has spent much time working in them knows, are usually too time-consuming to allow much experimentation with life styles. . . . I believe what motivates my generation is more a despair with the methods and the facts of the past than a new life-sustaining freedom and joy. When we consider the amount of change during our life-times, we cannot help shivering at the specter of a future of ever more rapid change.

A faculty member of a change project on the University of Massachusetts campus discussed at a conference for action-research teams how his group got started and the motivations which keep it going. It was clear to him that the primary source of energy for this successful venture came from the desire of faculty, students, and staff for a more personally satisfying experience; they were unhappy with their learning opportunities, with their professional development, and with their relationships. He says:

About two years ago a group of faculty from across the university would get together to talk. We had some common interests in organizational behavior and theory. Those talks were focused kinds of things. We would pick an area and get together to discuss it every other Friday. These sessions degenerated after awhile into bitch sessions about the quality of life and how much fun we were not having. Then we said, "We are applied behavioral scientists. Let's do something about it." From that emerged a process in which we finagled from central administration a faculty position which we filled with four off-campus people, each on a fourth-time basis, who really built a collaborative relationship. Out of that, we have grown to about sixty people, ten or fifteen faculty, fifteen or twenty staff, and a bunch of doctoral students, who form the Applied Behavioral Science Alliance, as it is called. . . . What happened is that we began to work on projects. We usually have a floating group of teams. For example, we did a workshop with the School of Nursing that totally reorganized it—from a discipline-based faculty to interdisciplinary teams. My sense of why the Alliance works is that the whole thing got initiated on the basis of self-interest.

It is possible, of course, to operate with the old verities, in the old styles. But many faculty are increasingly uncomfortable with those forms. They seek new relationships, new processes of teaching and learning, growth for themselves, and a sense of competence that flows from something more meaningful than laying the word on captive audiences.

Similarly, many students are seeking new ways of living and learning. Keniston (1968, p. 287) after a study of young radicals, concluded that these men and women are seeking a number of changes. Their goals seem to be shared by many students and faculty, particularly as Keniston points out, the most articulate, intellectual, aggressive, and successful students.

[They seek] new forms of adulthood, in which the principled dedication of youth to the betterment of

society can be continued in adult work that does not
require blind acceptance of the established System, but
permits continuing commitment to social change. . . .
They seek new pathways of personal development
wherein the openness of youth, its fluidity, growth, and
change, its responsiveness to inner life and historical
need, can be maintained throughout life. . . .
They seek new values for living, values that will fill the
spiritual emptiness created by material affluence. They
seek new styles of human interaction from which the
participants grow in dignity and strength. . . .
They seek new ways of knowing, ways that combine
intense personal conviction with relevance and enduring
adequacy to the facts. . . .
They seek new kinds of learning, learning that maxi-
mizes the involvement of the intellect in the individual's
experience, instead of divorcing the two.

The difficulty in achieving these goals in most institutions
is the cause of much distress; teams which can mobilize this distress
and transform it into actions can provide a worthwhile service both
to their members and to the institutions.

3

Blocks to Change and Responses

The campus is not quite an immovable object in the face of the forces for change that impinge on it from within and without. The barriers to change we describe below are not sufficient to block all innovative practices. New institutional forms are constantly developing as well as ways of meeting the dissatisfactions of campus dwellers and their desires for improvement. What we fail to see very often and strongly advocate is the merger of form and feeling in the changes that do take place.

Inhibitors of Change

Educational institutions have many blocks to innovation and creativity typical of bureaucracies. A key block is that schools prize order, rationality, predictability, and impersonal modes of operating. Grade point averages to two decimal places, class schedules to the minute, carefully circumscribed roles, stylized patterns of interaction, precise rules for earning credit hours, formalized processes for awarding tenure, detailed social regulations, computerized registration procedures, and complex requirements for degrees require highly controlled behavior. Change to some degree runs counter to orderliness and predictability; it can be planned and controlled but inherently it calls for new behaviors, different interactions, altered assumptions, and revised attitudes. One cannot always be sure where it will lead. That is one reason why self-correcting, action-research change methods are advantageous.

We shall now present a number of blocks to change on campus. First, however, let us note again that we realize there are many exceptions to our general statements. Nevertheless, the following behaviors are worth thinking about when one is trying to generate institutional change. For the most part, the issues that follow are organizational problems and tend to be dealt with, if at all, by structural changes which fail to address the reality of an emotional component. Action-research teams have the advantage of being able to meld emotional, relationship-oriented approaches with organizational, structure-oriented styles.

Difficulty of demonstrating value of change. Miles (1964) points out that it is usually harder to rationalize change in education than it is in business. There is no analogy in college to the profit-and-loss statement of a business to measure the value of a change. (We recognize, too, that the profit-and-loss statement is not as clear-cut a measure as one often pretends it is.) Klein (1967, p. 30) says "even in fields where results can be more or less objectively judged in terms of profit, recovery rates and the like, successful innovation occurs only after initial resistances have been worked through." It is no wonder that it is difficult to work through resistances to making modifications in educational institutions where measurements of values are exceedingly vague.

Even efficiency has a radically different implication in a college than it does in a business. Cost per contact hour is no way equivalent as a criterion to labor cost per unit in a factory. Obviously, one way to minimize cost per contact hour would be to put all Ohio State University students in the stadium on Monday, Wednesday, and Friday and have a $3,000-per-year teaching assistant lecture to them. There are, however, complexities in such cost reduction that do not occur in the manufacure of hub caps. The bases on which change can be initiated, rationalized, supported and evaluated in a college are much murkier than are those in a business. Such cloudiness makes hanging on to the status quo very attractive—particularly to persons who are comfortable with the present state of affairs.

Difficult role of the change agent. Jaques (1947, p. 61) summarized the problem of change agents in their dealings with those who run organizations: "In practice the problem boils down to the relationship between the 'expert' and the administrator or the executive responsible. We already know how difficult this relationship becomes even in the domain of the physical sciences and engineering; how much farmers, for example, often resent the intrusion of the government agriculture expert with his new and supposedly superior methods. How much more difficult does the problem of establishing a satisfactory relationship become, however, where not crops but the changing of human behavior itself becomes the target of scientific endeavor." Ambiguity about the purposes of education compounds this problem. Relationships tend to be strained between persons pressing for change and departmental enclaves of established power.

Bennis (1966, p. 105) sheds further light on resistances with which change teams must cope: "Human changes are bound up in self-image and its maintenance and the complicated context of the social life and groupings which help to define and give meaning to the individual's existence. . . . If an intended change is perceived as threatening the social life space of the individual, then safeguards must be undertaken whch ensure new forms of gratification and evaluation." Because of the social context to which Bennis refers, groups are often better change agents than are individuals. Colleges and universities, however, seldom provide much support for building collaborative teams.

Parochialism. An important impediment to innovation in most institutions is the parochialism which is encouraged by departmental organization. Theoretically, and occasionally in practice, units with a high degree of autonomy should be able to use their freedom to create imaginative solutions to problems. Often, however, conservatives are in power in nearly all areas of a university, and departmentalization distributes the change-oriented faculty so they cannot develop a critical mass.

Effective interdepartmental programs are rare, but many important tasks to which colleges need to devote attention do not fall within departmental limits. Therefore, change-oriented faculty in some institutions, such as the University of Massachusetts, have wisely taken steps to build interdepartmental networks of like-spirited folks to collaborate in trying to improve the quality of life in the institution. All groups in our campus change team project have been interdepartmental, and most of their projects have had an interdepartmental character.

Ambiguous role of administrators. The ambiguous role of administrators in universities or colleges makes it awkward for them to provide a clear thrust toward an innovative goal. Etzioni (1959, p. 53) describes the problem well when he states:

> The role of the institutional head in professional organizations constitutes . . . a typical case of institutionalized role conflict. On the one hand, the role should be in the hands of an expert in order to assure that the orientation will match organizational goals. On the other hand, organizations have functional requisites that are unrelated to their specific goal activity (obtaining funds, recruiting personnel, allocating funds). An expert may endanger the integration of the professional organization by overemphasizing the major goal activity, neglecting secondary functions, and lacking skill in human relations. Thus the role of head of professional organizations requires two incompatible sets of orientations, personal characteristics, and aptitudes.

Faculties, by and large, have not responded effectively to the dilemma posed above for administrators. They do not provide thrusts toward program modifications which would make institutions more growth-supporting and more enjoyable. Rourke and Brooks (1966, p. 129) note that "often in the past faculties have put themselves in the indefensible position of being willing neither to assume the burden of guiding a university's academic development nor to concede to others the right to do so." Project teams which include both faculty and administrators can help to achieve mutual planning and acting.

Lack of change-oriented concepts and skills. Institutions are seldom imbued with high levels of skills and concepts about change processes, a deficit that helps to block creative institutional change. Alternative strategies are frequently unknown to faculty and administrators—or at least they do not "know" about them in a way which affects their behavior. Organizational and change models employed in universities tend to be simplistic and power oriented.

According to Rourke and Brooks (1966, p. 14), "academic staff and administration were in effect playing a zero sum game in which gains for one side had to be offset by losses for the other." The ideas, values, and behaviors needed for collaborative problem-solving and cooperative innovative efforts often are underdeveloped. Thus, zero sum, win-lose games are played when they are not inherent in the situation. Action-research teams can reduce over-reliance on win-lose power strategies; they can increase the likelihood of using data-based, joint problem-solving styles.

Current activities "roll along." Another antichange norm is the strong tide in colleges and universities in favor of current practice—whatever it may be. Activities continue without serious review or evaluation. New programs are often submitted to unreasonable examination and expectations of advance proof of effectiveness, while old practices and programs which are questionably effective or clearly dysfunctional are continued without challenge. For instance, research data reported by Milton (1973) show that lectures are useful only for certain purposes. But no professor is ever required to demonstrate that lecturing is the best teaching strategy he can use. It is when a teacher wants to limit or to eliminate lectures that he may have to defend his teaching style.

Gardner (1963, p. 17) in discussing the tendency of the status quo to defeat innovation says: "When Emerson said, 'Once we had wooden chalices and golden priests; now we have golden chalices and wooden priests,' he was saying something fundamental about the relation of men to their institutions. We are forever 'building the church and killing the creed.' Form triumphs over spirit. A social institution is created out of human ardor and conviction. As its assets expand, the ardor wanes. The buildings grow bigger and the spirit thins out."

Change-oriented people not in main stream. Another block

to institutional change is the fact that change-oriented people are usually not in the institutional main stream; often they are in low-power positions—untenured faculty, staff of special programs, students, blacks, student affairs people, or assistant provosts in charge of innovative programs. Marginal people tend to be more change oriented, and one trick in promoting change is to support and utilize them. Havelock and others (1967, p. 66) note: "Some of the key functions in [knowledge] utilization are served by persons who are in intermediate positions between one professional in-group and another. Unfortunately, persons who occupy such positions are beset by many woes peculiar to this in-between status. . . . It is of utmost importance to understand their problems; and ultimately we must come up with solutions to their marginality." One value which teams provide is the opportunity for people to join together, to support, and to encourage each other in the pursuit of change. Marginality becomes less painful and threatening.

Discouraging policies and practices. Institutional policies and practices frequently inhibit change. For instance, an able young teacher at a university with which we have worked wanted to devote substantial energy to a group which was working on several institutional improvement projects. He was discouraged from spending much time with that group because it would not earn him any "points," and he was coming up for tenure. He worked instead on a research project in which he was not much interested and which he did not think was very good but which the department chairman wanted him to do. Similarly, students often must withdraw from change project teams because of the press of academic work and the inability to get institutional rewards for team participation.

Of course, most institutions have a whole jungle of procedures, forms, approvals, and permissions which stand in the way of any new activity. These bureaucratic processes may provide important control functions; they undoubtedly provide important blocks to change.

Competition of new activities with old. Another block to successful change activities is competition between new and old programs. If new forms show viability, those who invest in the current forms are likely to feel threat: if new acts squeeze into the arena, redistribution of power, money and other resources will follow. As long as the total revenues of the circus are increasing, new acts can be added without replacing old acts or reducing salaries of old performers. However, when revenues are falling, the old jugglers may fear the potential addition of a new high wire act.

One way to deal with this problem is to set up new acts in a side show where they can be used for advertising and promotion and to entertain a few folks—but they have to survive with minimal support from the company and have little effect on main events. Some side shows on campus are: living-learning centers, year-for-action programs, University Without Walls, independent study programs, off-campus projects, foreign study programs, and accelerated learning programs. Institutional improvement can be supported by developing teams or networks on campus and between campuses which link innovative programs. The self-defeating competition among them can thus be reduced; they can support each other; they can improve their diagnostic and action-taking skills.

Short academic life cycles. The school calendar and the life-cycle of inhabitants inhibit change. Most schools still run their core programs from September through May, necessitating the restart of a change group each fall. Even potent groups do not usually speed up before November. It is usually impractical to initiate new activities in the last few weeks of an academic year. What with examination periods, quarterly endings, and vacations, a campus team does well if it can have six months of fairly concentrated activity a year.

This short work space is further hard hit by the turnover of members: students at best have only a few years available, and faculty go on leaves and move to other institutions—making it crucial for teams to plan ahead to assure membership. These factors make continuity of effort over any extended period very difficult and put a premium on fast development of effective group processes.

Difficulty of maintaining volunteer efforts. Most innovation groups must cope with the always difficult problems associated with acquiring and maintaining the necessary energy flow from volunteers. Change efforts do not necessarily have to be conducted by volunteers, but college and university groups usually are voluntary, often totally, although sometimes there are a few members for whom the group involvement is counted, one way or another, as part of their work load. The volunteeristic nature of campus change teams means that particular attention must be devoted to seeing that the members build satisfying relations with each other, learn things they want to learn, and enjoy their membership in the group. If the rewards do not exceed the investment, the group will fold.

Having looked at some of the factors which inhibit planned change, we should point out that we do not assume every change is worth the effort. Not all changes are creative, practical, or improvements. Some people resist changes because they are correct in preferring the status quo. However, in view of the difficulties in producing *any* significant modification on a campus, it seems to us that there is a low risk of generating too much innovation. We have heard many faculty point out (while sharing wise looks), that there is no virtue in "change for change's sake." They seem to think they are combatting a real danger. Stability for stability's sake is the more likely hazard.

Responses to Problems

Programmatic. We became aware that there are a considerable number of programmatic responses to campus problems. New people are hired to head new programs; occasionally, someone is fired and a program is killed; more often, programs are allowed to starve slowly for want of love and bread. Programmatic responses thus can involve changing personnel; reorganizing the system; reshuffling roles; adding courses, curricula, or services; or reallocating space. For example, a programmatic response to the drug problem requires education majors to take a specified number of hours in a drug abuse course. But to us, program change approaches seemed frequently to fail to connect in a meaningful way with the personal distress of many campus dwellers.

Bureaucratic. Probably the most common attempts to change higher education are bureaucratic in approach. This approach consists of parceling out the various areas of activity—buildings, academic programs, student affairs, personnel policies, and finances—to specific parts of the bureaucracy which are responsible to a chain of command that goes up to the board of regents. The student is in effect divided along organizational lines: academic programs are developed by the faculty; counseling and the emotional lives of students are the province of the dean of students' office; dormitory construction and maintenance are the prerogative of the administration; and other kinds of functions are similarly allocated. Change is planned, carried out, and evaluated by the designated unit. Each area tries to dissuade everyone else from getting involved in its act. Persuading, disciplining, withholding information, giving directions, negotiating and using a consistently rational approach are typical modes of influence. The bureaucratic method is based upon concepts of efficient division of labor, chain of command, span of control, and organizational rationality—essentially conventional organizational assumptions. And essential to the success of this method is a capacity to maintain either a sense of fairness or discipline among the members of the institution.

Political. On a par in popularity with bureaucratic approaches to change is a political strategy that mobilizes critical power points into alliances which can muster enough votes to carry the day. Individual groups try to generate enough support to bargain for inclusion of their goals in the overall winning program. The primary focus is on identifying powerful individuals (as opposed to *positions* in the bureaucratic mode) who are willing to use their influence to support the cause. Trade-offs are made to maximize achievement of each participant's interests, but often there is not a total group commitment to the goal. The ability to identify the potentially influential and to find bases on which they can be joined is the essence of this strategy. Long used by administrations, faculty, boards of regents, and legislatures, this strategy tends to by-pass the student in terms of significant decisions. (But students have also relied heavily on political methods in their own governance.) Perhaps this lack of student involvement in institutional political processes helped to create the unease that developed the protest movement.

Organization and system building. These strategies provide other alternatives for creating institutional change. As universities have become big business, they have looked to industry and business as models of operation. Thus, during the 1960s there was a host of applications of management methods. Practices such as cost benefit analysis, management by objective, program budgeting, computerized financial controls, systematic goals setting procedures, and staff development programs have become common. These techniques often have been introduced as ways of better managing change as an everyday event; they often also have the appeal of controlling the rate of change and increasing predictability. The valued commodity is expertise rather than power or position. Often, change is accomplished by altering the procedures by which an institution works rather than by directly attacking the problem.

Protest and confrontation. Protest and confrontation came into their own on campuses in the middle 1960s, just prior to the beginning of this study. As Berkeley became a household word, reports of protest and confrontation could be found in most of the newspapers serving college cities, and such reports helped to spread the use of this method. Confrontation strategy rests on building a power base strong enough to disrupt the normal processes of an institution or at least create fear that there will be disruption. This power is then used as leverage in negotiations. Protest groups were often able to achieve some of their ends: more liberal student policies, altered institutional political stances, elimination of ROTC, and reordered priorities (on both local and national levels). The establishment, however, built its own defenses stronger, hired more security forces, tightened rules of conduct, and learned to mobilize quickly its own power. The consequence was that protest often resulted in violence and the movement toward goals was lost in debates about tactics. As Lewin (1951) points out, change tends not to last if it results from increasing driving forces without reducing any of the forces in the system which are set against the innovation. The history of many campus change efforts based on confrontation supports his conclusion.

Although revolution is a theoretical possibility, it has been used so infrequently in higher education that it is mentioned only to indicate the range of possible strategies. The basic thrust of a revolution is to overthrow the existing system and to replace it with a method of operating based on radically different premises. Approximations of this strategy are found in the development of alternative models, such as the Free University of San Francisco State in 1968, or of experimental colleges, where the values and methods are different from the traditional. These efforts, however, depend on the continuation of essentially the same system because they are in a sense branches from it, so they can hardly be described as truly revolutionary.

Other techniques. Institutions desiring change have generated a variety of specific techniques and approaches; some are identified here to indicate the range. Universities have developed institutes within their own structure, for example, the University of Cincinnati's Institute for Research and Training in Higher Education, which does internal consulting, knowledge dissemination, information collection and feedback, and departmental development. The Wright Institute has developed research, evaluation, and consultation services for programs in other institutions. These services are coupled with on-campus consultation.

Many institutions use formal means of collecting information about themselves and comparing it to data about other institutions: the Institutional Goals Inventory and the College and University Environment Scale are popular instruments. Action may be generated by feedback and use of the data in planning; the process is generally initiated and controlled by top administration, with occasional use of faculty and students. Faculty development programs have emerged on over 200 campuses; many work only with techniques such as audiovisual aids, but a few use group and organizational development methods. Associations (such as the Association of American Colleges, College Center of the Finger Lakes, and the Council for the Advancement of Small Colleges) have utilized workshops and on-campus consulting. Commissions (such as Carnegie and Newman) have done studies and made recommendations under the assumption that distributing information in rational ways will produce change. Pilot and demonstration projects (such as the University of Massachusetts Clinic to Improve University Teaching) are another approach to producing change. A particularly interesting project is Strategies for Change and Knowledge Utilization (an NIMH project under the Union for Experimenting Colleges and Universities, Saratoga Springs, N.Y.); it combines goal-setting, data collection and feedback, action-planning by an on-campus group, and use of expert knowledge in institutional improvement projects on eight campuses.

Individual Approaches to Change

In launching our campus change team project, we realized that many people on campuses were individually committed to working on change. These persons frequently were involved in activities calculated to improve their own and others' quality of life.

Living-learning centers, advising programs, self-directed studies, sensitivity training programs, and humanistic education projects absorbed their energies. Often we observed that these activities had low impact, had low survival rates, and were not joined together in a potent change strategy.

But reactions to dissatisfaction with the status quo can take a number of forms in attempting to improve the quality of life on the campus. One course of action is rebellion: strikes, demonstrations, sit-ins, unionization, and lockouts have been liberally used in recent years as techniques for rebelling against the system or some part of it. At the other extreme, individuals have discovered a number of ways to minimize their interactions with the system and to avoid efforts to change it. One is withdrawal. Currently popular withdrawal options are: forming alternative settings; dropping out; becoming a book worm, a jock, a party person, an individual artist; or turning to eastern religions. Another general course on which some persons embark is to try to move into positions in which they will be more influential and from which they will be able to build a more satisfactory life for themselves. Thus, people work at becoming star students, student body presidents, professors, deans, or committee chairman. Some join or create affectively oriented programs; others create or join a team which works at moving the system in the direction they would like to see it go. Such groups have the opportunity to deal with both affective and task-oriented issues, a mixture which provides rich interest and resources. The dissatisfaction felt by members is the driving force of the group. Groups which deal with issues directly connected to those feelings tend to be most active and tenacious.

Thus two channels through which persons in institutions try to deal with their problems in a positive way are: (1) the person-centered, relationship-oriented route (such as providing dyadic drug counseling), and (2) the task-centered, structure-oriented approach (such as adding a course). The structure-oriented approach often loses the motivation which derives from affective involvement. The person-centered approach frequently does not result in the social change which comes from organizational alteration. But we saw project teams as devices to tap the energy which flows from a personal, emotional commitment to an issue and channel it into programmatic responses which can have more impact on the institution; they can join the affective and the organizational modes.

Advantages of Team Approach

Figure 1 provides a visual representation of our concept of a project team. This framework relates to the work of Etzioni (1968), whose theory of guidance and control processes that enable social actors to transform themselves and his three elements of active self-direction (knowledge, energy, and power) provided useful insights for us. Raskin (1971) in searching for methods of social reconstruction as opposed to apathy, reform, or revolution identified similar variables. Both men discuss the role of "projects" as mechanisms to move from individual creative impulses to social action. Involvement in a project, as Etzioni says, literally "pro-jects" an individual into the social world. "Getting it all together" for these authors is not the act of an isolated individual—it is intensely social behavior that forms and shapes self-identity and transforms personal, group, and social spaces. The basic insight of these men is that individual and group efforts are interwoven in a project approach to social change.

The work of three other scholars should be mentioned in relation to the development of our concept of project or change teams. The concepts of Lewin (1951) are a foundation upon which we and many other behavioral scientists have built. Fundamental to the process we are presenting is his view of social systems as fields of countervailing forces that must be diagnosed prior to attempting any actions. He also heavily influenced the development of action-research as a change technology. Finally, we have relied on his emphasis on the importance of involving in the change effort those who will be affected by the change. Lippitt's (1967) ideas about the utilization of social research to improve social practice have been of particular value. Watson's (1967) theories about self-renewal mechanisms in social systems also have been integrated into much of our work. All of these concepts are woven throughout this book.

Personal, group, and organizational change can be mutually reinforcing but are limited by several factors. Personal changes are limited by group boundaries, such as the degree of openness and

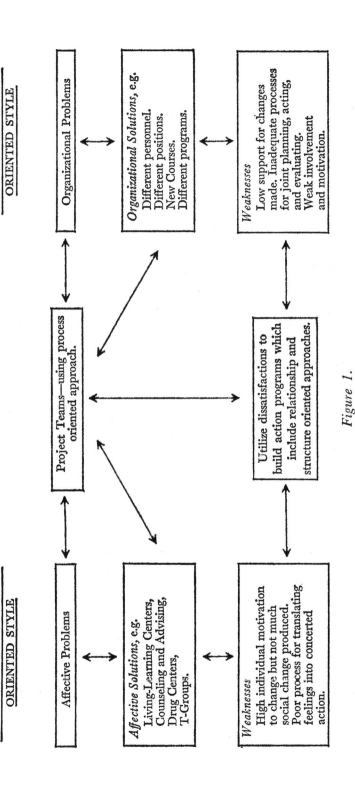

Figure 1.

PROJECT TEAMS—JOINING TWO STYLES OF CHANGE

sharing in the group and commitment of other members. Group change is limited by the structure of the organization that encompasses it and which may block or facilitate the group's capacity for change. (An innovative project might find a home more easily in an experimental college than in a traditional, authority-bound campus.) The action spaces of individuals, teams, and organizations are closely interrelated. The history and dynamics of the organization set at least short-term boundaries on its changeability. Change efforts can be supported by combining the resources of internal change teams with external consultants who provide help in training and research activities.

A basic problem, as we view it, is the low capacity of institutions for self-directed change in their own structures and processes. By self-direction we mean the capacity of the institution to be responsive to member needs as well as to provide opportunities for members to influence the institution. Campus dwellers generally are unable to join with others to transform campus life and to make it closer to their images and values. Although there is, of course, much individual intellectual activity on campus, social change is brought about by organized groups. Individual, group, and organizational skills are needed to generate the power for self-direction. Unfortunately, as higher education moves into the 1970s, with less share of the national prosperity and fewer students knocking at the doors, the campus finds the environment turning more malignant. The resources and attention needed to build the capacity for self-direction are more difficult to acquire. Yet higher education needs to tap the energies and resources of its members to make fruitful accommodations to the changing environment. Authentic participation by a greater number of persons and social units in the problems of the university would increase the institution's capacity for internal control by making more perspectives and energies available. Such involvement would also reduce the alienation felt by students and faculty and enhance the achievement of individual and institutional goals. (We hasten to add that this does not mean that we think everyone can or should participate in everything.) We believe that action-research change teams can help members of institutions to move toward more satisfying participation in institutional affairs and can bring about useful changes.

4

The Action-Research
Team Approach

Throughout this book we have been referring to the use of teams as effective agents to promote institutional changes. In the previous chapter we stressed their advantages in helping to overcome the problems and frustrations of campus life. Now we would like to give the reader a more complete sense of the kind of team under discussion by pointing out how it differs from other college action groups, such as regular appointed committees. You will find that teams of this type may be called project teams, action-research teams, innovation teams, process-oriented teams, or, simply, change teams. The terms are interchangeable, but a team of the type we are discussing has certain characteristics:

(1) It uses some form of calculated data collection and analysis for diagnosis and action planning.

(2) It consciously examines its own functioning.

(3) It basically is collaborative in its functioning and in its change strategies.

(4) It tries to implement change rather than merely make recommendations to others.

(5) The learnings and relationships of members are viewed as important and valuable outcomes.

(6) It often utilizes process consultants.

(7) It may be initiated in various ways: by administrators, by advocate groups, by departments.

Such teams have a number of strengths as agents of innovation: They can engage in a wide range of activities (such as workshops, survey-feedback processes, training groups, and intergroup activities); they can work on the learning of members, team-building, and organizational development. Groups which function well also maintain the interest and commitment of members. A team can provide a good base from which external consultants can work effectively with the college. Groups can acquire needed skills, attitudes, information sources, and experience by adding members. Long-range continuity of effort can be maintained by replacing departing members. Members can provide a wide array of valuable connections to various parts of the college system. A group can enhance the learning and enjoyment of its members. A team can provide energy for change and legitimacy for the change effort. Especially important is the opportunity for members to use the team to keep their courage and interest in working for change.

Process

In developing our project for action-research change teams, we were guided in part by the experimentation that had been done with students and faculty working together in teams in the NTL Institute Summer Programs in Higher Education. Their successes, as well as those on other campuses where we had consulted, contrasted with the usual failure of students, faculty, and administration to work creatively together. Because of their focus on building relationships and skills, we observe that such groups develop capacities to function well on significant tasks. Although this approach had not been widely used, a number of other models that had been used frequently were found wanting: Violent confrontations produced retaliation; traditional exercise of power left people feeling isolated and alienated; and student government, faculty senates, and administrative bodies (each doing its own thing) did not deal satisfactorily with many important problems which required joint efforts.

The campuses needed joint problem-solving efforts and new relationships to be built across traditional barriers. Active involvement in change processes was needed to avoid apathy, ignoring, or rebelling. A fluid process based on information, both objective and emotional, needed to be devised. To our delight, the campuses we contacted seemed eager and ready to experiment with the action-research team approach. The conformity of the 1950s and the radical dissent of the 1960s had laid the groundwork for the possibility of sharing of power among social units on campuses. Some top level administrators were receptive to the development of innovations at lower levels on campus. Students and faculty were attracted to these new possibilities for increasing their influence and learning new skills.

We felt that the introduction of participative organizational methods into higher education would follow the same path as they did in industry. Human relations technology was first introduced to reduce stress and alienation among the rank and file and to increase motivation, morale, and productivity. When the issue of exploitation of individuals was raised, more attention was focused on the ways in which individual enrichment could be attained as corporate enrichment was being pursued. As the value of this technology becomes increasingly evident to managers of higher education, we hope that values, goals, and power-sharing will be as subject to critical change efforts as are planning, decision-making, team development, and communication. If the strategy is authentically humane, it should make an institution more responsive to the concerns of all its members. The criteria for assessing the merits of this approach, then, must include these issues: the responsiveness of the institution to the divergent goals of its members as well as to the goals they share; the extent to which organizational goals are changed to actualize latent values of different members and subgroups; the changes in the underlying power structure that have been achieved; and the availability of energy to engage in productive conflict.

As with any other strategy, our approach represented an adaptation of a few basic themes along with the development of some special aspects that were particularly appropriate to the participating schools. The phrase *action-research change team process* says a good deal about our intent. By *action-research* we were committed to the notion that action in a complicated environment should be based upon the collection of information in a reasonably systematic way and that information should be used in assessing the impact of a program on the campus. It is important that the data include both information from members of the action-taking group as well as information from the environment which they would like to change. We emphasized gathering information openly, with a clear explanation of purpose, and making the results available to all concerned. This approach contrasts with a "through the key-hole" collection of information in which one tries to be as unobtrusive as possible. The hope is that increased openness and motivation to become involved in a change process will offset possible biases. We saw the concept of a change team as essential to involving individuals from different sectors of the campus and to enhancing the possibility of maintaining efforts beyond any given individual's tenure. Very few individuals on campuses can single-handedly introduce a significant change, with the possible exception of limited areas (such as a classroom or dormitory). The emphasis on *change* clearly focused the project on the introduction of new practices rather than on the maintenance of established activities. The word *process* implies a developmental activity, over time, which actively seeks the involvement of those who will be influenced by the change. Their involvement is based on a dynamic notion of the problem itself and the activities which might help to solve it. Involvement includes interaction within the team and between it and its environment.

In sum, we proposed a strategy of change that undergirded action with information about the team and its members and about the environment, especially the aspect on which the change effort was focused. We proposed developing a *critical mass* by basing the strategy in a team instead of an individual or a collection of separate individuals. We proposed an organic, evolving flow to the plan of action rather than adherence to a rigid preplanned pattern. Thus, we see the action-research team functioning to implement change itself, employing a collaborative style, linking to many parts of the campus, examining its own ways of working, and using data in setting goals and planning for action.

The action-research model we proposed was utilized only in part by some of the teams, possibly because of ambiguity in our presentation of the model. The design calls for both the consultants and the teams to act as participant observers and observant participants. The consultants also fed back interview and questionnaire data to the teams to stimulate discussion about their own processes and setting priorities for team decision-making and action. This action-research model needs to be fully articulated and communicated as an adequate procedure for project teams to follow. Our observations reemphasize the need for action-research to be collaborative and to include the client whenever possible in defining aims, in data collection, and in interpretation of results. The emphasis on data collection to guide diagnosis and action did prove useful to the teams in our study but it was not a simple process to institute.

Our project developed out of a desire to explore action-research team change strategy as it applied to a variety of problems on a number of campuses. Although a few earlier programs used student-faculty-administration teams and action-research methods, they had been short term and had operated on very limited resources. We wished to extend the scope of work in this area. The choice of this strategy was derived from an NTL Institute tradition of collaborative action; it did not emerge from a detailed comparison of alternative strategies.

Advantages

As we have already pointed out in Chapter Three, the action-research team has many advantages over other strategies which lack collaborative effort and often are ineffectual. In general, it provides an integrated approach both to learning and to change—two highly valued activities in higher education; teams continually explore new areas and develop new skills and at the same time effect a positive difference in the institution. That combination is satisfying to members: it keeps them motivated and helps to maintain a flow of energy into the project.

This method, which is information-based and self-correcting through continuous evaluation and feedback, contributes to a better definition of the problem and to more on-target solutions. Its self-correcting feature is particularly appropriate in a campus environment where change tends to take place rather slowly. This approach contrasts with strategies which are preplanned, packaged, and do not provide for modification as they unfold. Resistance to change, although always present, is lowered by basing the effort on commonly shared information, jointly developed goals, and mutually planned actions. The emphasis on collaboration minimizes status differences and helps to avoid having people feel excluded from the process. More power-oriented strategies, such as bureaucratic or confrontation methods, can often produce action more quickly than can project teams. The innovations, however, tend to be washed out in time because the resistances in the organization are not dealt with in a way which generates support from those who must carry out the new procedures. Teams also have the advantages of keeping attention focused on the problem area, providing a base from which outside experts can function, maintaining activity over an extended period, building connections within the organization, and developing members' change-related skills.

For most of the project teams we worked with, the major differences between them and regular committees were: formation of the team on the basis of members' interest; it was a voluntary effort, not an official assignment; selection of goals as well as means by the team members; equalitarian relations among the team members regardless of rank in the institution; an explicit focus on the processes and the dynamics of the team; an explicit focus on the needs of members, particularly affiliation needs; regular consultation; and membership in a network of teams that were part of the overall project and participation in interteam meetings.

We cannot be sure which of these ingredients were responsible for the results we are reporting, but we did attempt to evaluate the total process of change, including the contribution of the consultants, by asking the participants to compare their experiences in the project teams with alternative procedures in the same institutions. Teams operated for periods ranging up to four years so that fairly long team process-and-outcome evaluations can be made.

Member Evaluations

Here are the taped comments of three team members who attended our retrieval conference in November 1973. Their observations were of value in helping us in the final evaluation of the project, particularly in regard to individual achievements and development.

Finch (University of Massachusetts) : The whole thing got initiated on the basis of self-interest. There was a lot of talk about doing things for other folks but what it really boiled down to was doing some things for ourselves. The basis of the project was self-interest, personal growth, professional growth and development, sharing relationships, finding out what was happening with other people, those kinds of things. And then as we began to really work, I think some other things happened. For instance, when I go to work on another project, I have some definite and clear expectations: that I be able to engage in research while I am doing the project. It usually is a joint kind of thing where the research is of value to the people I work with but I get some extended knowledge in making better sense of various ways to work with organizations and improve their effectiveness. Also I get to bring graduate students and doctoral students so they get a chance to do some field work. I think if those things can be built in, the problem of the investment of time seems less of a problem because you build in your needs rather than working for some outside altruistic purpose.

Delone (College of the Virgin Islands) : In terms of the role of NTL being the external force. . . . Now it is a different situation in that it was not paid for by the college and did not serve to legitimize the team in that sense. But it provided us with some very important mechanisms by which we can evaluate ourselves and become more aware of each other and develop better interpersonal skills. These were all things that were very important in the long run. . . . The personal development and personal interests of the people involved was the most important thing that kept the team going and that kept the members committing themselves. So initially we started out with very simple tasks so that we knew we could accomplish something in a very short period of time and that people would say, OK, this is

a little bit different than other committees because we
can get things done and that was a basis for getting people involved.

Howard (College of the Virgin Islands): Before
I came into the team I had confidence in myself. I was,
and still am, an independent person but I never expected
to see myself in a leadership role. My experience with
the team has helped to bring out certain qualities, helped
me to assume a leadership role.

Change Objectives

The long range goal of our work is to increase the capacity
of institutions of higher education for authentic, collaborative, self-
direction. Our immediate objective in the project that inspired this
book was to support and study teams on campuses which were trying to use an action-research approach to innovation. Such project
teams have the following objectives that are individually familiar
but innovative in combination:

For individual team members our objectives included: increasing knowledge and awareness of self, team, and conditions on
the campus; increasing commitment to convert feelings and values
into action; extending skills and power to realize goals; increasing
integration of the capacities to plan, to develop resources, and to
exercise influence; and improving skills in initiating and participating in team projects which involve collaboration with other team
members.

For the action-research teams our objectives included: co-
operatively developing and using knowledge and imagination in
designing a goal; mobilizing and utilizing assets and resources such
as time, money, and people; conversion of resources into power to
realize team goals; establishing links to other parts of the campus;
and collaborating with individuals and social units on campus who
are affected by the change.

*For the institution of higher education our objectives in-
cluded:* opening up aspects of the institution for discussion and
increased understanding; mobilizing activity to carry out specified
and agreed-upon change projects; increasing links between knowl-

edge specialists, people committed to causes, and people in power positions; and spreading the project team model by initiating additional projects with wider membership bases and broader concerns.

These objectives describe the move from personal to group and organizational self-directed change. We attempted to increase the capabilities of individuals and groups by consultation, training, and research. In addition to helping to develop an action-research model, we tried to increase member commitments to the team's task—especially important since most members were volunteers. The strategy for increasing the commitment of members included helping the group to focus on sharing member feelings and concerns, emphasizing personal involvement in selection of goals, caring about each member's personal and professional development, establishing realistic goals, and emphasizing the building of teams in which members like and enjoy one another.

Strategies

The general strategies used by the teams can be divided into three categories, although teams used more than one of them: being advocates of specific reforms, acting as links between conflicting groups on campus, and operating as organizational change agents. We will elaborate on these strategies as follows, using enlightening comments from team members.

One team which had just experienced student dissent on campus saw themselves as links to facilitate communication between administration, faculty, and students. As they said, "Work to give students the tools to get to the administration and give administrators "ears" to hear students. . . . Add a new constellation of membership and resources to provide linkage from one part of the university to another—administration to students or vice versa. Try to serve as a bridge between faculty-student-administration. . . . Is there a danger of change teams prematurely smoothing over a crisis? Yes. . . . Don't cut off confrontations, provide resources to make them constructive."

Another strategy teams used was to advance specific reforms. The members of these teams advised: "Don't select initial projects that confront power. . . . Initially select highly "do-able," short-term projects with a high potential for success. The team needs feedback that it can do things, such as a workshop. . . . Build in success and show the connection of a small success to long-range goals."

Other teams operated as organizational change agents seeking to use collaborative consensus as a way of reducing resistance. They told us: "Don't look at your adversary as a person with some human qualities, but as a human who is also an adversary. . . . Don't try to give help to a client group that doesn't want it."

One strategy everyone all agreed upon was how to convert failure into success: "Failure and review equals a learning experience. Make what went wrong right on the basis of learnings." In a sense, they said that there is no failure if there is learning. In other words, change is a risky business. People who participate in a change project need to be prepared to deal with failure in a way that prepares them for the next innovative effort.

The teams' links to the campus were especially important strategically, according to team members. They warned against the dangers of the team becoming isolated: "The team should be aware that they have to establish linkages with other parts of the university. Don't be too self-contained." They also emphasized the need for accurate appraisal: "Assess the climate in the institution. For instance, what is the attitude toward change and the specific change effort in the institution? Identify the helping and the blocking factors." Team members stressed acquiring resources from the campus: "The change team has to be aware of energies in the environment and how to use them." Finally, the teams were aware of the dangers of alienating power figures: "The real power is with the faculty, you may not need their support, but don't alienate them."

The comments of two team members who attended our retrieval conference illustrate how working on the action-research project showed them that they could get things done by working together with other people, despite opposition.

> *Diaz* (University of Puerto Rico): The power issue came from the beginning. It had to do with the motivations for people to join the group. Some of the

goals that we set out implied taking away the power from the director of the department. We had a big power struggle with her and then we decided, shall we say, to evict her from the group. We couldn't integrate the group with a big power figure. The other thing we discussed here was our self-image. As the group progressed, at some times we were not sure of where we were and what we could accomplish. . . . Gradually with some things we did, our self-image improved. Another thing was our relationship with the consultants . . . and how we were so anxious in the beginning to please NTL and to have something to show when they came to visit us. Now we feel we grew in the sense that we could develop our own purposes and ask the consultants to help. In terms of the future, we have grown to the point that we want to continue the project and we are seeking some funds to continue the research activities. Included in the funds are help from the consultants to help us go on.

Vincent (University of Utah) : It is kind of interesting when you look at it, in the context of the committee being part of the educational process of the institution, that a change team notion fits into a total concept of teaching students, and faculty for that matter, how to work through bureaucracy, how to get change.

5

Case Histories of Teams

Now we will present short histories of the teams which were in the campus change team project and also a more detailed description of the University of Massachusetts Applied Behavioral Science Alliance, which will begin this chapter. Each case was written by members of the team and presents their views of the group experience. Subject matter and style were selected by the case writers. The basic work in preparation for writing the histories was done at our November 1973 retrieval conference at which there were representatives from each team. Those who attended the conference are noted in the preface to this book. William Kraus also worked on the preparation of the history of the University of Massachusetts Applied Behavioral Science Alliance although he did not attend the Conference. These case histories clearly illustrate the variety of potential successes—and pitfalls—that can be experienced by teams as a whole and by individual participants.

A Campus Change Network: University of Massachusetts

In 1971 and 1972 a group of two dozen faculty, professional staff, and graduate students from various areas within the university of Massachusetts met at regular intervals, initially to explore a common interest in organization behavior and change. Soon, however, the discussions turned to critiques of the quality of life at the university. From these discussions emerged the Applied Behavioral Science Alliance, an organization committed to improving the lives of faculty, staff, and students.

Formation. Included in the initial group were fifteen to twenty faculty members from the schools of business administration, education, nursing, and psychology; some graduate students from the same disciplines; and a few professional staff from the student affairs group. By fall 1971 it became clear that the group had common concerns about university functionings. At one session it was noted that the administration was making available a limited number of "pool" faculty positions to be used exclusively for interdisciplinary efforts. A subgroup of six people decided to attempt to get money for one of these positions to use for support of what was to become the Applied Behavioral Science Alliance. The money would be used to pay for consulting and workshops and a variety of change projects on campus.

Contact was made with Vladimir Dupre, president of the NTL Institute, to explore possible ways of collaborating with NTL in a change effort at the university. After a series of negotiations with NTL and with the university administration, a faculty position was secured; four one-fourth-time people were selected to fill it.

The goals of the project were identified as: (1) developing a collaborative relationship with NTL which would make the broad resources of that Institute available to this campus; (2) promoting internal collaboration at the University of Massachusetts among people and programs with common goals and interests, particularly to reduce divisions among academic programs, student affairs efforts, and administrative offices; (3) exploring and modeling a process of collaborations both within and outside the institution; (4) applying behavioral science knowledge to undergraduate populations as follows: faculty teaching improvement programs and faculty self-renewal, contribution to living-learning environments, and experienced-based learning opportunities; (5) enriching the available resources for the professional development of faculty and students; (6) modeling a process of self-examination; (7) promoting development of theory and practice in applied behavioral sciences through graduate student and faculty research, and program development in various campus systems; (8) promoting interchange with other behavioral science efforts at other institutions.

Achievements. These are the major accomplishments of the first year and a half of the Applied Behavioral Science Alliance:

The September 1972 workshop: The core group which initiated the project decided to expand its membership and develop a network of resources throughout the university. Fifty to sixty people were invited to attend a three-day workshop for the purposes of goal-setting, team-building, and planning for the future.

The School of Nursing project: The School of Nursing project provides an example, which will be presented in some detail, of the way the Alliance works. During the September 1972 workshop, a small group of nursing faculty identified the School of Nursing as a subsystem which could use Alliance resources. A number of problem areas were identified and project teams formed (all of which included School of Nursing faculty). For example, the administration of the school agreed to a two-day workshop for its faculty to reorganize members into interdisciplinary teams so that faculty organization would be congruent with a newly designed curriculum. One off-campus faculty and seven Alliance members from other departments designed and facilitated the workshop. The nursing faculty reorganized themselves and dealt with several issues which derived from their previous history and the reorganization. Subsequent consultations and workshops for the School of Nursing included: (1) a three-day residential student-faculty workshop to learn about organizational change and interpersonal dynamics with forty-five senior nursing students and seven nursing faculty attending; (2) several Alliance members working with nursing faculty as cotrainers to increase faculty skills in facilitating the personal growth groups which were a part of the new nursing program; (3) a two-day workshop designed and facilitated by five Alliance members to explore and resolve current problems in the school, with design of a new faculty decision-making mechanism as its major outcome; (4) an Alliance member acting as a consultant to the School of Nursing faculty team to negotiate a merger with the Department of Public Health.

Other projects: Other Alliance activities were as follows: a two-day problem identification and planning workshop for the School of Business; work to improve the quality of life in a large high-rise dormitory; a series of seminars and consultations with the staff of the health service; consulting about planning with the dean and department chairmen of the School of Engineering; facilitating the merger of two departments in the School of Education; helping a group of black graduate students to develop applied behavioral science skills; consulting with the staff of the Center for Institutional Resource Improvement; helping with the formation of a collaborative network of student affairs staff members; trying to build better links between special programs; development of an interdisciplinary organizational development curriculum; seeking ways to support antiracist and antisexist efforts; consulting with the staff of the university press; providing workshops on alternative ways of teaching; and conducting professional development and planning workshops for the Alliance.

An overall effect of the Alliance is increased permeability of the boundaries between university subsystems, for example: team teaching by faculty from different academic disciplines; student affairs staff and doctoral students teaching courses together; graduate committees formed with greater interdisciplinary representation; formation of interdisciplinary faculty support groups; increased visibility and acceptance of Alliance members in many parts of the university; increased collaboration between several teaching faculty and student affairs staff; recognition among Alliance members of a large pool of university resources for personal and professional growth and development; and increased visibility and legitimacy in constructing alternatives to the traditional teaching/learning model.

It is clear that the Alliance has provided an opportunity for the creative development and sharing of resources and for significant outcomes that would not have occurred without its presence.

Functioning. The Alliance functions by members identifying a problem which they want to work on, gathering resources from within the membership to work on the problem, and proceeding with problem-solving activities. The major method of problem identification is that one of the off-campus faculty [consultants] are contacted, either by Alliance members or by individuals within the university community who want help. A project is initiated if other members are interested in working on the problem. Other projects have been initiated by members of the university community who request assistance. Alliance members also see problem areas and initiate activities to deal with them.

The Alliance is a voluntary organization, and formal organizational rewards do not accrue to members for their involvement. The rewards that members receive are the opportunities to acquire new skills and knowledge, to work in satisfying ways with other university community members and the off-campus faculty, to engage in action-research, to make improvements in the institution, and to provide graduate students with an opportunity to engage in practical training right on campus. Needs for inclusion, affiliation, affection, and mutual support are also met by the Alliance. There are about 120 people in the Alliance, about forty of whom are actively involved.

The off-campus faculty are essential to Alliance functioning. They come to campus as a team three days each month. For Alliance members, they serve as catalysts in the generation of ideas and projects, consult with project teams, and assist in action steps. Since they are not members of the university and are widely seen as experts in the area of organizational change, they have access to parts of the university which are unavailable to on-campus people.

There have been several recurrent problems. The first relates to the addition of new active members. Most new members come to meetings because they are intrigued by the excitement communicated by a highly involved member. They usually come expecting to learn new skills and to be closely involved with powerful individuals. These expectations usually are not fully met—a lack of clarity about the organizational functions and how one gets actively involved can be confusing. Prospective new members are told that working on projects is the only way to become involved beyond attending the monthly meetings. They may identify a problem they would like to work on and draw from alliance resources, or they may link up with an existing project team. Both alternatives are difficult, the first because it is time- and energy-consuming and the second because teams which have already formed find it difficult to integrate new members. (The Alliance has not found a totally satisfactory way of recruiting and involving new members.)

The second major problem with Alliance functioning involves its leadership and administration. A variety of mechanisms have been tried to establish decision-making, communication, leadership, and to handle the variety of necessary administrative tasks. These leadership mechanisms have included task committees, a rotating leader-of-the-month, decision-making by exception (decisions made by a few are automatically implemented unless objected to), no differentiated leader, emergent leadership, and a volunteer leadership group which is open to anyone who wishes to invest time and energy in running the organization. The Alliance in spring 1974 functions under the latter mode, the most satisfactory model to date. At the beginning of the second year, an Alliance member on the university staff had the responsibility of coordinator for the Alliance built into his job. None of these methods for providing leadership have been totally effective. Given the ambiguity of Alliance functioning, the rejection of hierarchical values and acceptance of collaborative values, leadership is a tender issue.

It is essential that faculty be centrally involved. At the core of Alliance functioning is a group of faculty who have devoted a great deal of time and effort to initiating and maintaining the organization. The bulk of these faculty, however, have professional school associations. Few liberal arts faculty have been involved and few projects in these areas have been undertaken; this has been a major shortcoming of the Alliance.

Another chronic issue is the large extent of time and energy involved. The central administration of the university and the subsystems to which members belong have not, for the most part, recognized Alliance membership and the work members do as a legitimate part of their roles. Time for work on Alliance tasks must therefore be squeezed out of other activities. In some instances, members have withdrawn from the Alliance because of pressure. Often members are highly conflicted over their involvement in the Alliance because of other demands. The most powerful inducement for continued involvement in the Alliance is a sense of commitment and the caring of core members for one another.

A major issue concerns short-term successes. It is vitally important for a voluntary action-oriented organization to experience success. Obtaining the faculty pool position, engaging the services of four outstanding consultants to staff the position, and working on a variety of projects have provided essential successes. Short-term goals were set as steps to long-range achievements, but there is still frustration at a lack of impact on the basic organizational processes in the university.

Finally, a crucial issue has been where within the university should the Alliance devote its time and energy. Its focus of involvement has been largely on the periphery of the university; mostly with professional schools, the student affairs group, and special programs. The Alliance has not resolved the issue of how to generate maximum organizational impact. The question has been: shall the Alliance attempt to change the essential core of university functioning—the way the faculty is organized and operates, the traditional teaching/learning process, and the central administration of the University? An explicit decision *not* to become primarily involved in these areas was based on member commitment to collaborative values, an unwillingness to become involved in the hierarchical power process, an interest in working on specific change projects, on feelings in and out of the Alliance that the Alliance was in a low power position, and on the fact that there have been few overtures from potential clients in those areas.

The Alliance has had a significant impact in those areas to which it chose to devote its energies and has achieved important short-term success. However, the central administration and the faculty and administration of the College of Arts and Sciences who have the greatest voice in the continuance of the pool position do not for the most part understand the goals and functioning of the Alliance. In times of shrinking resources it is natural that the Alliance faculty position has a low priority. If the Alliance had decided to work in more central areas, knowledge of its goals, functioning, and the resources it makes available would probably be clearer. The consultants make available an excellent opportunity for gaining entry into the central administration but the Alliance has not fully capitalized on that potential.

Improving Student Services: College of the Virgin Islands

The Student Affairs Team of the College of the Virgin Islands (cvi) is a volunteer group of administrators, faculty, and students. Its general purpose is to establish itself as a change agent by providing training in group dynamics to its members and by utilizing problem-solving techniques. Fred Thomas, dean of students at CVI initiated and organized the team in fall 1971. At that time his main concern was to create a team to bring about positive campus change in student-faculty relations, to develop student leadership, and to make student personnel services more responsive and effective. The criteria for selecting team members were: membership had to be representative of the college's multi-ethnic setting; candidates had to demonstrate some potential for leadership; candidates had to be motivated by personal concern for the betterment of student life.

Approach. The team has employed a problem-solving approach which consists of problem identification, diagnosis, evaluation, action steps, and follow-up procedures. A main underlying principle is the belief that collaboration between administrators, faculty, and students will aid team-building and problem-solving. Team structure has been organized to facilitate student leadership training. For instance, students have been encouraged to coordinate the team's activities and to chair meetings. They have also been encouraged to head subcommittees comprised of administrators and faculty.

By the end of the first academic year (1971–1972) the team had firmly established its problem solving-procedure and modus operandi, which were task activities undertaken during that year. Initially, the team was concerned with student-campus welfare problems (such as inadequate walkways, lighting, telephone service, and recreation hours for the field house). As the team "jelled" and became increasingly successful, it took on such problems as curriculum development in the physical education department, development of independent study projects, and improvements in the registration process. As a result of this work, the administration officially recognized the team as a problem-solving group and encouraged students to become acquainted with its functions. In the second academic year (1972–1973) the team continued with the projects from the previous year and added studying the cafeteria service, improving preregistration, and participating in workshops

with an action-research team at the University of Puerto Rico
(UPR).

The first NTL workshop with the UPR team in fall 1972 led
to several significant events. For example, team members had a negative reaction to working on data collection for research purposes.
They were fearful of losing their task orientation. They also felt
that interpersonal encounters were a waste of time and preferred to
"get on with some action." The overall result was a strictly task-
oriented operation. Six months later, however, at a similar workshop in St. Thomas, team members became interested in developing
interpersonal skills. Since that time, the team has been progressively
moving toward a greater integration of task, interpersonal, and
group processes.

Confrontation. Upon returning from the Barranquitas,
Puerto Rico, workshop in Fall 1972, the team concentrated on its
own development and temporarily reduced its involvement in task-
oriented activities. The team felt that its problem-solving action on
campus would be greatly hampered without support of the general
student body. At that point, the team was under attack by student
council leaders who felt threatened by the team's activities. The
team focused on recruiting and orienting new members. The recruitment campaign was a direct answer to rumors which had been
circulated on campus by the student council regarding the closed
membership of the team. A regularly scheduled student convocation
session was used to present the team's policies to the student body.
It was well known that one of the student council's complaints concerned the selection of students who attended the Barranquitas workshop. At the convocation session, a faculty member and two students
presented a promotional speech to recruit new team members. At
first the convocation session was very disheartening. The members
were subject to heckling and unfair accusations. They were not
given a chance to respond to questions. The team's relation with
the dean of students was at the core of much student aggression
against the team. As a result of this opposition, the team increased
student membership, achieved a closer attachment among team
members, and did the groundwork for better relations with the
student council. Unfortunately, several old team members dropped
out.

Less than a week after the confrontation at the convocation session, the same students who took a vigorous stand against the team organized a sit-in at the college library to protest the conditional contract offered to a black faculty member. The administration could not cope with the situation and used police force to remove students from the library. This was a very critical event in student-administration relations. The dean of students was caught in the middle and the implications of this event were to effect his position and the team's at cvi. This confrontation concluded the first academic semester of the 1972–1973 school year.

At the beginning of the second semester the team turned its attention back to tasks, although it continued to discuss further team development and evaluation. The effects of the Barranquitas workshop had worn off. The campus was faced with student apathy as a result of the administration's suspension of students who were involved in the December sit-in. A student, Kay Howard, volunteered to act as team liaison with the student council to keep them informed of team activities. Thus, the team would no longer be accused of being a closed group. Team activities for the spring included: investigation of the need for a student snack bar, organization and sponsorship of a student-faculty beach party, and a voluntary faculty student tutoring plan to assist students before final examinations.

Early in the second semester (February 1973) we had a second NTL workshop with UPR on St. Thomas. The workshop served to reinforce team relationships and to orient new student members. We also discussed the problem of campus communications, campus apathy, and what the team could do to improve the situation.

Shortly after this workshop, our membership was again bolstered by the addition of a faculty member, a student-affairs staff member, and another student. To improve student-faculty-administration communications at the college, the team cosponsored with the student council a beach party for the entire college. Its success indicated of how far the team had come since the first semester in its relations with students. The well-attended beach pary was a feather in its cap.

At the close of the spring semester (June 1973) while Fred

Thomas, dean of students, was attempting to obtain funds to send several team members to Bethel, Maine, for an NTL workshop, he was relieved of his position. His persistence at obtaining the funds for the workshop may have been the immediate cause of the administration's sudden move, but the underlying reasons for the decision to eliminate the position had developed throughout the year. Thomas's stand during and after the December sit-in was a particularly critical factor. Needless to say, his removal had serious implications for the team. During the summer a faculty and a staff team member received much feedback from the administration to the effect that the team must be disbanded.

Regeneration. The team's future was unclear as the fall 1973 semester began. Initially, little was said or done to reactivate it. However, the election of two team members as president and vice-president of the student council revitalized the team: one of the most significant plus factors in the team's history. It was hoped that the action-research model and group dynamics training learned from participation in the team would be used by them in their administration of the student council.

Once again the efforts of Fred Thomas got the team rolling. He could not have done this without the continued interest and support of team members. Much of the motivation behind his reinitiation of the team's effort was the fact that NTL was planning a workshop in St. John, Virgin Islands, for early in the semester and it would include members from both the University of Puerto Rico and CVI. Again the workshop played a key role in the continuation of the team by facilitating the participation of new members in the development of new goals and objectives. New members were impressed with the UPR team, the setting in which the workshop was held, and the general management by the NTL consultants.

Upon return from St. John, energy was generated to get the team back in action, a process necessary at the beginning of every semester. The first project to receive attention was the possibility of creating a radio station on campus. Team members also indicated an interest in arranging for workshops aimed at developing group skills, and in utilizing the skills of various professors and college personnel. It is hoped that the benefits of the workshops can, eventually, be passed on to the student body and the community via the student council. With the departure of Fred Thomas as well as other key team members, the team needs to develop a structure that will guarantee its existence by building a foundation for continuity.

Involving Students in Decision-Making: University of Utah

From 1970 to 1974 the University of Utah participated in an NTL project designed to study change, action-research, and the behavior of a group involved in a change process. Several administrators, encouraged by the NTL project director, provided the main impetus for starting this committee. The group which participated in the study became the Resource Committee on Student Participation. It was created to encourage and to support behaviors on the part of faculty and students which would enhance the effective utilization of newly created departmental student advisory committees. The group drew its faculty via appointments by the academic vice-president's office and from the student body via the student government: Associated Students of the University of Utah. The executive secretary in the last two years was a member of the student affairs staff.

Because this change in student involvement in decision-making had been mandated by the university senate, the committee was not initiated to create change but rather to assist in the development of a change in process which had been started. This proved to be less than some members of the committee aspired to as change agents but the group's activities flowed from a fairly simple, low-key reform posture as opposed to a radical stance.

The departmental student advisory committees were designed to provide student input on decisions of tenure, retention, and promotion of faculty. It was also expected that the committees would assist in constant evaluation of curriculum and suggest new courses to complement the educational experience. Prior to establishing these committees there was no significant student activity on the departmental level at the university. As the departments attempted to implement the policy creating departmental student advisory committees, there was no existing structure for student recruitment and, in the early stages, the committees often were comprised of student friends and supporters of the departmental chairmen. This pattern was not typical as the groups matured. Once functioning, committees found themselves involved in a number of activities beyond the original charge. They became student associations and have provided a great deal of student programming on the departmental level of the university.

The Resource Committee on Student Participation served well in the role of feeding the development of the departmental student advisory committee system. The committee's occasional research in the strengths and weaknesses of the advisory committees stimulated students and faculty. This stimulation occured both at the time of research interviews and when the data were distributed. The university now has some type of student advisory committee in every department. Through this research the Committee discovered a number of action steps which it could take to assist the development of the departmental student advisory committees. Most successful were the publication of a departmental student advisory committee handbook and a series of departmental workshops. Both projects were funded primarily by student funds with support from the student affairs group. The success of the departmental student advisory committees was also supported by the tenure review process in which the administration constantly asked for the departmental student advisory committees' reports.

The Committee will now be disbanding. The original task of developing the departmental student advisory committees has been accomplished. Future maintenance of these committees has been accepted by other elements of the university. In total, the project was successful; it clearly was a device of the administration to implement the departmental student advisory committees—and it worked.

Throughout the existence of the Resource Committee on Student Participation, a number of problems plagued the group from which significant learning can be drawn. The Committee often failed to recognize the importance of personal rewards to group members; periodically all work on the project stopped while the Committee worked on personal concerns of its members which had not been dealt with. Some faculty members felt their membership threatened their tenure achievement; others used the Committee solely for prestige or for personal payoff. Student turnover resulted from students being limited in their time at the university and also from the Committee's lack of progress, at times, toward goals which were significant to student members. (Several students, however, were members for two or more years.) The most important learning centered in the realization that personal and professional development were as important as the task; both agendas had to co-exist as a basis for group achievement. The group found its greatest success during the two years when staff members and students directly charged with the success of the departmental student advisory committees because of their professional or student government assignments became members of the team. The personal payoffs of the group's activity centered more on accomplishment of the task during this period.

NTL commitments to the project and interest in the group members were of great assistance; perhaps they were key to its survival. The Committee found that with changes in administration, leadership, and frequent membership turnover, the outside consultant provided the real continuity for the project. (At one point the Committee had but one member who had been just recently recruited.) Credit here should also be given to Dr. Virginia Frobes, who as dean of students primarily initiated the Committee. Though her role at the university changed several times during the years of the project, she constantly supported the group. She served for a time as a Committee member, and while chief student affairs officer, provided university funding to the group. Undoubtedly the vision of student involvement she holds was served by the Committee. And of the many people who served as members of the Committee, she was the most enthusiastic in the evaluation of the group's success. Since group members did not select either the overall goal or the other members, the feeling of success is less widely shared by the individual Committee members.

The outside NTL consultant to the Committee not only provided it with continuity and resources but also was primarily responsible for the group's behavior pattern. Through frequent participation in NTL-sponsored workshops, members of the groups were converted to the NTL methods which concentrate on group behavior. (It should be noted that the NTL consultant frequently worked on helping the group to set goals, organize for work, plan, design strategies, assign responsibilities, and moniter its progress.) Particularly in the first two years, the group often would lapse into periods of emphasis on relationships and self-awareness to a degree that interfered with its task achievement. Some members freely admitted that the project was no longer of any interest to them but the group interaction and personal caring about the other members became their reason for staying with the group. At the retrieval conference in the fall of 1973, the Committee shared with the NTL teams the observations and the learnings it would give to others attempting a similar project. One conclusion that the Committee highly recommends is the use of a consultant.

Increasing Relevance in a Psychology Program: University of Puerto Rico

The Action-Research Team at the University of Puerto Rico was created in spring 1970. During the preceding fall and winter Dr. Sikes had proposed establishing such a team to various university deans and to the faculty, students, and staff of the psychology department. The first broad purpose set for the group as it came into being was improving that department. Persons who were interested in the project joined the group and included the department director. Five faculty, one staff member, and five students, in addition to the director, became the team. University administrators continued their early support of the team—an important asset.

The team had difficulty establishing early operational goals. At the suggestion of Dr. Sikes, a one-day workshop on goal-setting was held in April. At the workshop, attended by Dr. Sikes, a good deal of time was devoted to dealing with team members' suspicions about the consultants' motivations for establishing campus change teams. Several students suspected that the project was a CIA cover to use in spying on campus groups. These suspicions were laid to rest after considerable discussion; from that point on the relationships between NTL and the team were close, warm, mutually rewarding.

The team established curricular reform in the psychology department as its general goal. In May 1970 the group attended a workshop for all the teams in the NTL project. Prior to and during that workshop the following more specific goals were agreed upon: to change the curriculum to prepare graduates for professional tasks; to make students conscious of Puerto Rican social problems; and to make teaching more relevant to the real problems students will face.

A research design was roughed out for gathering information to help work on these goals. During the summer, however, little work was done and the team entered the following school year at a low ebb. Early in the fall, the team decided to change its task to departmental planning and development. After initial support for that change in focus, the director reversed her opinion, which caused much distress. However, the team then reaffirmed its interest in curricular reform and continued research in that area. Data collection subgroups were established; they interviewed employers, designed and administered a questionnaire to alumni, and interviewed faculty and current students.

At this point the team obtained $4,000 from the administration to help support the research and other team functions. The team extended its knowledge and visibility through the research project and was very pleased with its progress.

Throughout the life of the group, the main motivation and satisfaction of members were derived from the personal growth opportunities and the interpersonal relations among members. A recurring issue was whether or not to recruit new members. This question was resolved in favor of bringing in new people and a process was set up to do that. Many new members then joined from time to time and were fairly easily integrated.

In spite of the team members' excellent relationships with each other, there were several persistent problems. One related to sex roles and was uncovered when the chairman, who was one of two men in the group, resigned because he did not like dealing with so many aggressive women. There were also on-going differences over power relationships in the group. Students were periodically suspicious of the genuine willingness of faculty to share power. From time to time some members felt others were being bossy or pushy. These concerns were worked out by open discussions. A more difficult problem, however, was the team's relation to the department director. The group felt the director was blocking them from effective action; ultimately the team asked her to withdraw. (Shortly thereafter under faculty pressure she was removed as director.) Another difficult problem was deciding how to finish up, to report, and to use the research. The team finally resolved these issues, wrote a report, and devised a strategy for generating action from the data. First attempts to communicate research findings to the faculty were not successful, for the faculty felt the team was too much of an elitist in-group concerned with its own life and that it was manipulated by the director. Subsequent presentations of the report to individual faculty members and discussions of action steps with them alleviated this problem. Additional groups of faculty and students were created to work on specific problem areas pointed up by the report. The report was also used by faculty and administration in various program planning activities.

Several team members attended NTL human relations laboratories and gained personally from these experiences. In the third summer a group of six was sent to a two-week NTL team training program in Bethel, Maine, where they designed a strategy for implementing the changes indicated by the research. After their return, the whole team did not accept this plan with high enthusiasm; this disinterest, coupled with a strike at the university at a crucial point, caused the plan to fail in most respects.

The team next experienced one of several periods of depression. Often these periods were due to external factors (such as riots, strikes, and closings of the university) that blocked progress. There were also recurring doubts about whether the change efforts were worthwhile and whether the group strength was adequate to produce the changes. The workshops and visits from consultants which NTL provided helped to pull the team through several of these low periods.

Its comprehensive research report which has been used as the basis for a number of actions by the team and others, resulted in several curricular changes, some alterations of teaching styles, a new advising program, a different decision-making process in the psychology department, and improved relations between students and faculty.

The team's most exciting achievement has been creating a program of using students in four mental health centers on the island: the team selects and trains student workers and student supervisors. A grant of $15,000 was acquired to pay students who need financial aid, and others work as volunteers. The program combines a rich learning experience for students with service by the university to the island population. It is a long step toward the goals which were set up by the team four years ago: creating educational programs which have social utility for the community and provide more useable skills for students.

Improving Instruction: Lesley College

In the fall of 1968, Lesley College (Cambridge, Massachusetts) began what was to be a five-year liaison with the National Training Laboratories, a project which was designed to be beneficial to both parties: The college would form the Action-Research Group with a specific goal, and NTL would get information for its own research on campus change groups.

NTL approached the college administration with the idea, and under the leadership of the dean of students the team was formed as follows: At a general meeting, approximately forty students and ten faculty were given information about the project; and after discussion, a steering committee of five was elected to choose members for the team. It started by surveying all students and faculty for interest in the project. The criteria for selection were: the group was to represent all campus subgroups, both formal and informal; and within campus subgroups, influential persons would have preference. The steering committee then selected thirty nominees, each of whom was interviewed before the final selection of a ten-member team was made.

The team had its first meeting in spring 1970 with all but one member present—a faculty member who soon resigned without taking part in the group. After spending a good deal of the day's meeting discussing goals and direction, another of the faculty resigned because of a strong desire to work in an important area other than the one which had been chosen as the team goal: the improvement of instruction.

Shortly thereafter, NTL sponsored a workshop for the teams at Manresa-on-Severn, Maryland. Its purpose was to help build strong teams by working on group development. At this point the team realized that the steering committee's effort to achieve broad representation had resulted in few personal links within the group— a fact that was to cause many problems as the project progressed.

In fall 1970 the Action-Research Group began to work toward the improvement of instruction. The team interviewed eighty students and faculty about their instructional concerns and reported the results to the college community. The team then organized an open student-faculty meeting to discuss the report and to set up action groups to work on particular areas of concern. Seven groups were initiated at the time, each with a "maintenance person" from the team. Two important results came out of work in this area. First, a committee from the liberal arts faculty was established to investigate and propose changes in the curriculum. (Two team members were on the committee.) Second, of the seven action groups, one, the intellectual climate committee, whose intent was to arrange cultural events on campus and to raise the level of cultural consciousness in students, continued to work throughout the year.

In the fall of the second year, NTL sponsored a second get together, this time in Coolfont, West Virginia. The group, which then contained only five of the original members, worked primarily on team building and personal growth of members.

The team's next course of action was the development of a comparative course evaluation to rate faculty performance, hoping that through this device faculty would be encouraged to improve instruction. The survey was distributed, administered, and tabulated. The top four courses were identified in an article in the student newspaper. Faculty reaction to our endeavor was mixed, with negative feelings predominant. Faculty suspected that individual results had not been kept confidential as promised and that the survey instrument had been poor. There were few noticeable positive results.

After the evaluation it became more evident that there was strong need for liaison between students and faculty to deal with academic problems. The group decided to set itself up as an academic counseling clinic. Clients were solicited through advertising in school publications and word of mouth. There was little response from students or faculty; the clinic's only business came through team members and was quickly exhausted.

Shortly after the demise of the clinic, the liberal arts curriculum study group published their report—which immediately met with stiff opposition. The importance of this report and the resulting proposal spurred the team into action. The full report was published in the student newspaper, and the team distributed clippings of the report to each student. Wide student support was gained at an all-student meeting. The team organized a student "write-in" to faculty expressing support for the proposal. This quick action resulted in the faculty voting overwhelmingly in favor of the reform, but they directed a lot of anger toward the group for so-called "pressure tactics."

The next NTL-sponsored conference highlighted for the team the awareness of the need for more personal growth and group development. The team was continually reevaluating its goal. Team interpersonal conflicts between members were often discussed but not dealt with. The problem of dependency for leadership in the coordination could not be resolved. The NTL consultants were most helpful with content issues rather than with the interpersonal ones that the group tended to overlook.

The fall of 1971 started off a new year, new members, and a "kick-off" NTL conference for teams from all schools in the project. Flagging motivation and tight schedules allowed only the coordinator to attend. Since in the following months time became a major problem, the coordinator (an administrative-faculty member) solved it by sponsoring a course called "Leadership in Planned Change" in which all members could enroll. This move provided the group with at least the course time to meet and plan. And students were rewarded by earning academic credit for their efforts.

Due to the registration and scheduling process, students who were unaware of the group already were enrolled in the course. This exacerbated the continuing problem of member integration. As part of the course, the class decided to implement a second course evaluation using a well-established and less controversial model—the Purdue Rating Scale for Instructors. In light of faculty response to the previous survey the team adopted the following procedure: each member was matched with several faculty on the basis of affiliation; faculty were individually approached and asked to participate in the survey; and arrangement was made for Purdue to process results and send individual results to individual faculty (only a total read-out of the overall averages would be sent to the team).

It was discovered that students rated faculty fairly high, averaging 76th percentile on Purdue norms. Faculty who refused to participate, however, expressed anger at even being asked, which demoralized team members who approached them. Some faculty—only those who scored high—later approached the coordinator to discuss their results as compared to the average. Some of these same faculty shared positive results with administrators. Many faculty in conversation seemed to assume that the coordinator was given the results regardless of the promise of confidentiality. The team was unable to see any positive instructional changes resulting from the survey.

At this point the group disbanded. Group process continued to be overly dependent upon the coordinator. Low energy, mixed commitment, some confusion between viewing the group as a course or a project; and the varying views of its success all contributed to the decision. At its last meeting, it also developed that graduations and other factors meant that no student would be able to continue in the fall. The group was dissolved with reluctance but relief.

As of this writing, the administration has instituted a regular process to evaluate courses and faculty performance.

Changing a Grading System: University of California, Davis

In January 1970, initial contact with campus administration at the University of California, Davis, was made by NTL Project Director, Dr. Sikes, and university administrators supported the formation of an Action-Research Team. In April, the dean of students, Van Richards, invited members of the campus community to participate in a project "centered around the relationship between student life and the entire area of academics." As a result, a group of about twenty students, staff, and faculty formed a loose action-research team to work on reducing student stress. The next month five team members attended an NTL workshop in Annapolis, Maryland. Team-building and goal-setting were emphasized at the workshop. The team's target was redefined in June: "to investigate and work for change in the advising and counseling programs on the Davis campus." When the dean of students left on leave of absence, Lynn Bailiff, an undergraduate in applied behavioral sciences, assumed coordination functions for the team. He and Trish Reid attended a two-week NTL workshop in August.

After the fall term began, the team planned and conducted an open workshop regarding the individual and stress in the university; twenty-five people attended that October meeting. The team's target was again redefined: "to work for changing the campus grading system which generates stress that strongly influences the lives of those within the campus community." Team members undertook areas of research regarding students' attitudes about their transcripts, alternative forms of transcripts used at other colleges and universities, and institutional blocks to changing the transcript.

The following month, six team members attended an NTL workshop in Berkeley Springs, West Virginia. In December team members distributed a questionnaire they had devised—"Students' Attitudes Regarding Their Transcripts"—to a randomly selected sample of 500 undergraduates. The results showed large-scale discontent with grading and the transcript system. From this material, the team assembled "Casebook Regarding the Transcript." Copies were distributed to all team members. In February 1971 the team held a meeting with six significant members of the academic community, deans, and members of key academic senate committees, to test their responses to the idea of grading reform. As a result, in April Lynn Bailiff was appointed to a subcommittee of the academic senate committee on educational policy that was charged with evaluating the present grading system and recommending appropriate improvements. The only activity worthy of note during the fall was the attendance of ten team members at an NTL workshop at Round Hills, Massachusetts.

During January-February 1972 the team planned its strategy for supporting the subcommittee's intention to recommend changes in the grading system which the team believed would reduce non-productive stress. The subcommittee recommended substantive changes the following month; its proposal was endorsed by the committee on educational policy and sent to the members of the academic senate for consideration. In April, Bailiff reviewed the literature concerning the implications of grading for learning. His report, "Grades and Grading," was distributed to campus administrators and all fifty members of the representative assembly of the academic senate. An article supporting grading change was written by Sarah Woerner, team member, for the campus newspaper. Next, team members called individually on about two-thirds of the members of the representative assembly to discuss the proposed grading changes. Other concerned members of the campus community were enlisted to help in this project, forming the committee for improving education. But in May the assembly voted down the proposed changes: seventeen "for" and twenty-four "against."

A follow-up survey in June to members of the assembly, "Academic Decision-Making," revealed that the team's efforts at persuasion were significantly less influential than were the assembly members' personal experiences as teachers and as students. As a result, the team faded into oblivion as its members pursued other interests. The problem is still unresolved: the academic senate has considered and rejected grading reform twice since May 1972.

Providing Human Relations Services:
State University College at Buffalo

An Action-Research Team was formed at Buffalo State (New York) in the fall and winter of 1969–1970 after it was selected to participate in the NTL project. The team first focused on the problem of academic advisement. One area of interest was the state of advisement of "uncommitted" students. Several faculty members on the team shared this interest, which was supported by the students and soon expanded to deal with a broader range of problems. This was a period in which peer counseling and street drug programs were beginning to develop. As a result, the team decided to try to start a help center. This decision was made at an NTL workshop in spring 1970. The group then became quite cohesive. The help center was to be a 24-hour call-in and drop-in peer counseling program that was to deal with a broad range of problems and concerns that people presented. In summer 1970 Jim Beckley and Dick Meisler submitted a proposal, which was funded, to the state education department's program for the prevention of drug abuse. The proposal presented the help center idea as a response to drug problems on campus but it did not limit it to drug-related concerns. The project was formed in fall 1970 with a training program for student volunteers conducted throughout the fall and winter. After a good bit of bureaucratic wrangling, the help center was set up in the spring of 1971.

Getting the grant from the state education department was a critical and very important event which provided further validation of the group and its mission. The Action-Research Team was very distant from the prevailing philosophy of the college administration. This distance was most evident in the team's search for a physical location for the help center. The director of the counseling center and the vice-president for student affairs used this issue to express their reservations about the help center, even though they had expressed nominal agreement earlier. The question was resolved in a political confrontation. The support received from members of the office of the vice president for academic affairs was more powerful than was the opposition of student affairs people. A good location and the right to implement the help center concept were won. In this period faculty participation was largely symbolic; general support and the greatest action inputs came from the students. The group was close-knit and familial; it clearly provided members with a primary group experience that was not available elsewhere on campus.

For a period, the team tried to manage the help center. Several students who were active volunteers at the center became members of the team, but this effort at integration was unsuccessful: they never were assimilated and did not understand the background of the project and the norms of the group. The team had failed to structure itself into the help center as part of the management in a workable way or to provide it with realistic structures for self-management. The team, perhaps unwisely, cut the help center loose to sink or swim. It had a very vital period but after about fifteen months it sank. The team's failure in the management area was related to the battle it had to fight to establish the center. That period was highly political and difficult. It seemed impossible to do the job of establishing the management of the center properly and to win the fight at the same time.

The team then moved on to a period of discussion of a wide variety of campus problems. Many problems were related to the general quality of human relations on campus, especially race relations.

Although the group had a long-standing interest in race relations, it originally had no black members. A black dean, Leb Arrington, made a gradual entrance into the group. One of his first actions was to pressure the group to demonstrate real concern about race rather than to express mere concern. This factor was important in the group's decision that its next project would focus upon building a new format for a course in interpersonal relations. The course was to deal with more students than were typically in a class and was to have a stronger focus on race relations.

During the spring semester 1971–1972, Arrington began to take more of a leadership role in the group. He brought into the group four or five new people who seemed more oriented to task activities than were most old members.

In June 1972 six members went to Bethel, Maine, to attend the NTL laboratory. They brought back a number of action steps, including giving workshops that would address themselves to general problems on the campus (such as communication and human relations). Several subcommittees were set up to begin working on specific workshops.

In October 1972 half the team attended an NTL workshop in Coolfont, West Virginia. The group had expanded to twenty-six people. Subcommittees were set up to plan workshops for administrators, for united student government, for the black liberation front board, and for sexism. Arrington was elected director of the group at the Coolfont workshop. Carol Reichenthal was elected associate director, and an executive board was selected to make specific decisions. The group felt that decision-making had become too cumbersome as a result of the size of the group.

After returning from Coolfont, the executive board began to meet once a week, and the large group began to meet every other week. Decisions made by the executive board related to when consultants visited the campus, budgetary matters, and new groups that wanted to become a part of the team. A decision by the executive board *not* to admit a group interested in drug abuse produced a great deal of controversy. A heated discussion in meeting after the decision culminated in the executive board's deciding to reconsider. The drug committee was subsequently invited to become a part of the team.

In December 1972 a three-day workshop was conducted by the team for the united student government organization and the black liberation front board. The precipitating factor for holding the workshop was an intense conflict with racial overtones. The conflict was modified tremendously, if not solved, and the perceptions of individuals who participated were changed. That same weekend, the sexism subcommittee gave a sexism seminar that was covered by TV, radio, and newspapers. In February 1973 the team held a two-day administrators workshop that included the president, vice-president, associate vice-president, deans and other administrators of the university. Its primary accomplishment was construction of bases for communication between participants. (One thing that is lacking in this team is adequate follow-up of workshops.) In February 1973 the drug committe gave a concert-lecture. The subcommittee constructed and handed out a questionnaire to determine the extent of drug abuse on campus. Only sixty of the approximately 400 people returned the questionnaires and the usefulness of some of those was at best questionable.

In March 1973 the team sponsored a three-day workshop on campus with three NTL consultants. Approximately twenty people participated. A primary issue dealt with the relationship between the executive board and the team. The executive board was viewed by some as a power group. This question had been asked a number of times, "How does this group get off making decisions for the whole group?" There was resentment because the executive board meetings were closed and some members felt that they were not having enough input. These issues were at least partially resolved at the workshop.

In June 1973 five people attended the NTL program at Bethel, Maine. As usual, those who went to NTL came back very inspired and ready to move—there was quite a bit of energy in the group during the August and September meetings.

In October, the group had a two-day workshop for the purpose of firming up goals and preparing for a team workshop that was to be held in November with two consultants from NTL. The group decided that the workshop focus should be on acquiring improved skills and techniques for designing, planning, and implementing workshops. The president, two vice-presidents, and some deans also attended segments of the four-day workshop. The team's purpose in inviting them was to gain more support and to make them more aware of what it was doing.

In November nine members had a part in designing and facilitating a very successful workshop for eighteen students involved in the student assistance service, a program similar to the now defunct help center. The program for the group included process groups, crisis intervention, self-awareness exercises, and a presentation on counseling and referrals. Several team people are working with the student assistance service on an on-going basis. At present, workshops are being planned for security, the united student government, the resident assistants in housing, and the minority training leadership program. A new subcommittee, the student involvement group, is also very active at this point. The dean of humanities has consented to be chairman of the administrators workshop group. The group had thirty-five active members at the time this support was written.

Developing Teams on a Changing Campus: Antioch College

Antioch College opened in October 1969 a Washington/ Baltimore campus with a program center in Columbia, Maryland. The major goal of the new campus was to set up an educational process which was different from the soup kitchen model of education where disinterested teachers pass out watery pap to bored students. As the program's proponents noted in a brochure, students were saying: "I'm tired of being taught by teachers who don't want to teach and being in classes with students who don't want to learn"; "I'm sick of repetitive courses taught by professors willing to lecture and preach, rather than conversing with students on an equal level"; and "I don't like separating my academic life from my life in general."

The new campus aimed at achieving student participation in the means as well as the goals of their education: connecting learning to social action; learning by problem-solving, using the surrounding institutions and people as learning resources; and providing opportunities for students to work and to study concurrently. The students took an active role in developing the structure and functions of the campus; many were part-time administrators. They also were active in building the curriculum and devising the teaching and learning methods.

Many students arrived at the college frustrated by their experiences in high schools and other colleges and excited about a campus where they could "do their own thing." At the same time, many were uncertain about how to employ that freedom. Some students wanted more structure to the campus; others decided to wait until they got their heads together before becoming involved. A number became fully involved in the development and design of the new learning environment. To promote the work-study continuity, and to meet the rising costs of education, many students worked twenty to forty hours a week. They lived in small apartments and townhouses dispersed throughout the community. The faculty tended to reject the role of teaching subject matter and concerned themselves with helping students to find educational opportunities in jobs, projects, books, seminars, discussion groups, research, and applied science projects. They wanted education to be personal and connected to the realities of the world.

Michael Metty, director of Antioch/Columbia Center for Social Research and Action, was instrumental in setting up the first NTL-Antioch Action-Research Team. With encouragement from NTL, Metty and some students created the team to study the development of the college as a living-learning community and to devise ways of improving achievement of the goals the community wished to work toward. The team was composed of volunteers and was open to any community member, although potential members were told that some continuity on the team was desirable. The group seemed eager and anxious to get started. Soon, however, the consultants noted that the group was easily bored, did not feel meetings were accomplishing much, and responded to boredom by restlessness and leaving the meetings.

The team early on engaged in developing a questionnaire designed to find out how people in the Antioch community were spending their time. Metty supported the idea and provided some help in designing the questionnaire. The students committed themselves to carrying out this project and displayed a high degree of energy in formulating the questionnaire and in planning its implementation. Unfortunately, the team's skills were not sufficient to design and carry out such a complex data collection program. As the project bogged down, the group turned from high enthusiasm to near collapse. Discussion concerned feelings about the project. Many uncertainties were expressed about the values of the information for decision-making, the representativeness of the sample, and the difficulties of analyzing the results. The obvious lack of motivation to complete the project was linked to members' inability to see relationships between findings and anything they really wanted to know. The members who had completed their interviews were angry at those who were not fulfilling their commitments. The energy of those who wanted to continue the project was not sufficient to carry the burden. The team dissolved, but its failure generated a significant and widely spread learning experience: people who wanted to meet their own needs had to find ways of getting together with others to form reasonably stable arrangements.

The team that formed in the second year was somewhat more stable and more concerned with task accomplishment. It turned from monitoring institutional progress to preparing the college for accreditation. The group wanted to achieve accreditation in a creative way that would have a favorable impact on the institution. This task was seen as an opportunity for the team of students and faculty to learn more about the college and to institute improvements. The team felt it was doing an important task and satisfaction with the meetings was quite high.

A core group of students was committed and active but they lacked time to complete all of the activities and they also lacked skills in setting priorities for use of their time. The team was highly dependent on Metty who helped them to develop working procedures. He assigned tasks to people and got reports on progress. Overdependence on Metty was helping to get the job done but, as he was well aware, it had serious liabilities for developing an on-going team and was personally very wearing. The team members felt they were the only effective working committee on campus. However, it was not clear what mandate they had for action steps to be taken beyond gathering information for accreditation. Although the team began to see many needs for action, it had no clear understanding of how action oriented it should be, or what goals to focus on.

Ironically, in contrast with the objectives of "personalizing" the educational process, most motivation was associated with the task of accreditation. Members sensed that their activities were approved by the rest of the campus; they felt powerful as they went about their job and attempted to influence other committees and groups on the campus to get their jobs done. The team also developed greater understanding of how the whole institution operated. Yet the members, for the most part, worked individually, with little collaboration and little colleagueship from other members of the team. In sum, team members viewed themselves as performing an important task for themselves and for the institution. They were personally highly committed to the project and saw their team as being fully supported by other colleagues, students, and faculty. But they were concerned about time and priorities and saw little need to develop stronger intrateam relationships and skills. When Metty was assigned to another project and left the group it fell apart rather quickly. However, the members did report that their team experiences and NTL workshops helped them to work better together in other campus leadership roles.

The team developed some ingenious ideas for the accreditation report but it was not able to finish the task. The job of completing the self-study report for accreditation review by the North Central Association was turned over to a professional writer. The review committee was impressed by two features of that report: some novel ways of presenting the school and inclusion of students in the report preparation. Both features are now in the accreditation guidelines.

The last team at the school was building a new program to train mental health workers. Paul Shoffeitt and two student assistants, Margaret Ferguson and Gregory Alter, were the core people.

The goal of the team was to develop a new model for persons who were already working as paraprofessionals. The ingredients of the program were competency-based modules and a variety of resources that students might use to equip themselves with the skills and knowledge required by the modules. The overall concept was exciting and challenging. At the same time, the program was poorly connected to its students, as a result mainly of their heavy work loads as mental health paraprofessionals. The program was inadequately connected to the local environment, other programs, and the overall director of the center. The new venture had to compete for resources in an institution which was having serious financial difficulties. Despite the high commitment and shared values of Shoffeitt, his two chief assistants, and some of the students, the problems of gaining resources and implementing the program were overwhelming. Support for this kind of training from the National Institutes of Mental Health was being cut off, which compounded the problems. The program was incorporated into Antioch's Human Ecology Center where some of its concepts and methods are preserved.

The program director and his staff felt the NTL consultation was helpful in making the transition out of their program into another. It afforded the team a new and helpful context in which to face the issues confronting it. The consultants represented reality, and their objectivity brought new insights into the nature of the difficulties the program was encountering and suggested alternate action strategies. Meeting with another team at a workshop helped team members to understand that the problems they were facing were not unique, which reduced some of the feelings of desperation and frustration. Being part of a larger process, the NTL project, was experienced as beneficial.

Although the program which emerged was less complete than it was initially envisioned, the group did accomplish its goals. A community mental health training program was established and institutionalized. The program director saw this accomplishment as a reasonable compromise between his original ideals and the troubles which plagued the team.

6

Putting It All Together

From the team case histories reported in the previous chapter, the reader can see how easily change efforts can flounder in face of strong outside opposition and member discouragement. To insure success, certain factors must be considered in selecting any type of change strategy—whether the action-research team approach, organized protest, revolution, or bureaucratic or political action.

Selecting A Change Strategy

First, it is critical to be clear about where the mandate for the change effort comes from and what it includes. The mandate is, in effect, a charter for setting up the operation. Generally, action-research derives a mandate from both the formal power structure in the institution and from those who will be affected by the change: both groups approve the project, support it to some extent, and are willing to make resources available. In protest or revolution, by contrast, the mandate comes from a group which is not in formal power. In bureaucratic strategies, the mandate need come only from the hierarchy. Political movements maintain mandates by building networks of interest groups through tradeoffs, compromises, and appealing to a core of common values.

Another crucial factor is the degree and type of involvement of those who are engaged in the change effort. The bases for involvement can be: power, skills, information, representation, courage, or energy. Action-research teams put a premium on skills, energy, and broad representation and participation. Relevant skills are in data collection, analysis, interpersonal competence, planning, and knowledge about social change. The political process involves in central roles those with power, influence, and connections. Bureaucracies like to have well-defined groups which have responsibility for a specific activity with little involvement of outside persons; involvement in planning increases as one rises in the formal hierarchy.

The decision-making and conflict management processes also differ. Action-research teams systematically gather information, solve problems through consensus-seeking, and encourage broad participation in decision-making. Decisions can be made by people from all levels. In contrast, protest groups generally have strong, centralized leadership; they actively generate conflict with authority and reach decisions by negotiation. Typically, persons at the bottom and at the top are engaged in this process. In bureaucracies, decisions are normally made high in the pyramid and are handed down. Conflicts are normally dealt with in rational modes (such as job and role changes, reorganizations, explanations, and orders).

Targets of the change effort must be considered; that is, the persons who must change if the goal is to be reached. Political or protest strategies often focus on altering behaviors of specific individuals or getting acquiescence from a person with formal power. Action-research teams tend to use a more problem-centered approach that involves the target groups in trying to reach solutions. In bureaucracies, change theoretically (and usually in practice) flows from the top down with subordinates as targets—they are expected to conform to instructions and orders.

Although we believe action-research teams are a good agency for many innovations, we do not assume they are best for all circumstances, for their success will depend on conditions to be discussed below. Sometimes bureaucratic or confrontational styles may be more effective. In other cases, perhaps a revolution is called for. One should let the conditions determine choice of strategy; but we think that opportunities for collaboration often are lost because of lack of skill or faith in the task. Project teams can help to extend the use of collaborative styles, which we believe are healthier for individuals and organizations in the long run.

Conditions for Success

The success of an action-research team depends upon the existence or creation of the following conditions which support the process.

Most critical, perhaps, is a fair degree of common values among administrators, faculty, and students about issues of participative action, sharing of power across different levels of the hierarchy, and the resources which are appropriate for the change project. Unless there is an understanding that minimizes disagreement over power and control, it is doubtful that a collaborative change program can be sustained. *People in power must be willing to be influenced by the process.*

The complexity of an approach which includes data collection and involvement of those influenced by the change makes it important to have a stable group operating over an extended period of time. About three years is normally required for a project team to produce significant innovations. Experiences with campus change where crises were chronic (including strikes, critical financial difficulties, key personnel shifts, and high turnover among students) have demonstrated the difficulty of moving ahead in highly unstable conditions. All change groups need the ability to modify plans and strategies in response to new conditions—but a continual necessity to cope with crises seems to make planned change impossible.

The availability of time for team development and action is essential. The inclusion of significant personal development goals as well as the attainment of institutional change means that the team must spend considerable time in developing cohesion, trust, and the skills of group members. Commitment to recruit and sustain members and to developing links with other relevant campus interest groups also takes time. The collection and analysis of quality data on most campuses cannot be done very quickly; teams need to understand that reality.

Teams also need a fairly high level of tolerance for conflict, since most significant campus change counters someone's self interest; resistance to change is almost universal. The likelihood of conflict and resistance necessitates good channels of communication among the interested parties. Appropriate forums and procedures for managing and resolving conflicts are of great value.

Our experience with campus change indicates that the degree of stability in the environment is an important influence on a team. As we have mentioned, where crises are chronic, planned change efforts are difficult to sustain. At the other extreme, where the institutional style is overdeveloped and rigid, self-directed change efforts are not encouraged. The optimum environment is one where there has been a steady rate of change which has provided acceptance of innovative efforts with enough stability to lever off.

In general, change teams should be expected to aim for long-term effects rather than to fight fire. The expectations of accomplishment should also be reasonable in relation to the available resources. Unrealistic expectations of a large return from a small investment can be the source of future resistance to innovative efforts. Large-scale change requires multiple, long-term, and extensive efforts. Project teams can be an important ingredient in such an overall effort.

Problems Encountered

Since so many things can and did go wrong with change groups in our project, these member comments from the retrieval conference are enlightening.

> *Slattery* (Lesley College) : What went wrong? It began with the composition of our group. NTL came to the administration, and the administration decided it would be a good idea to have a change agent team on campus and that instruction was what was needed to be improved most. So the group was set up with the goal of improving instruction. So they set up a rather complicated but carefully structured method for selecting the members of the group. Our principle was to have a broad representation. We wanted people from as many

different groups on campus; and we wanted people who were otherwise connected into the network of the institution, besides just being members of the group, so they could be double change agents.

At the time we thought this was a superb way of setting up the group since now it was a group that had all kinds of informal influence and power on the campus—representative groups of faculty, students, and administration. However, members of the group did not know each other for the most part, and group development was a fairly serious problem. In addition to that, our goal for the improvement of instruction was somewhat vague and susceptible to a variety of strategies. It possibly led us to a serious error. We regarded students as our clients, generally speaking, but when you go around improving instruction, you work with faculty a lot. We went around and worked with faculty as if they were our clients; and in fact, they had not asked us for any help and did not want to be our clients. We ran into a lot of negative response from faculty every time we offered to help them improve their instruction. In terms of our actions, we were successful in achieving a number of our subgoals. . . . But at each of those achievement steps that we could have regarded as successes, the negative reaction of the faculty that followed each one was so severe as to throw us right back into the dumps as if it had been a failure.

We found developing the group as an interpersonal growth group was quite difficult. Finally, one of our difficulties may have been my position in the college, as being very well connected with a lot of the system. After the first year, all of our members were students but myself; dependency on me was a continuing concern of the group. We were never adequately able to handle that.

Meisler (State University College at Buffalo): One of the interesting things for me is the two phases of the action-research team: basically, when I was on the team and then when it moved on to Leb. He and I have very different styles and the team had very different lives during those periods. In the first period, I was a

new person at the institution. The team was a way for
me to get some status, to get some support from people
who wanted help. It was a way for people who wanted
to get identified with some things that I was trying to
do to do that. It was a way for a little affinity group to
form. We were very strong in terms of the kind of support that we offered to each other . . . a kind of
internal team functioning. The maintenance stuff makes
you feel good. We were very weak in terms of our connections to the institution and in terms of our access to
power. . . . Leb has a way of making connections with
power and facilitating those connections. He has a way of
getting people in and having the group expand and
bring people in with additional concerns. The other side
of that is, with the increased size and with the kind of
focus on those sorts of things there have been some
troubles in terms of keeping the group on-going and
keeping the connections among the group strong enough
so there is some real life. In a sense, recently, the group
is getting to the point where it has the best of both
worlds. It is structuring itself in such a way that the
private payoffs of friendship, personal development, and
professional development are being combined with the
organizational payoffs, such as making the connections
with power and expanding the size of the group. That
has been an interesting pattern. That is very pretty to
me. I like the picture. We have made a lot more progress
than I thought we had. An organization must both maintain the personal payoffs that are required of a voluntary
organization and at the same time it has to be developing external relationships and its place in the institution.
There is another thing that interests me. For the kind of
collaborative thing that is required in a faculty, student,
administration venture, it seems to me you have to create
a culture that is unique for people to live in temporarily
when they come together. It has to be a mixture. An
accommodation has to go on. One of the important
things, as Leb has said, are the off-campus things that
shake people up, get them out of their normal environments in a way that the group can develop its own cul-

ture . . . I think the faculty are the most difficult to try and make a dent in.

Bailiff (University of California, Davis): Some of the issues that we identified are: We tackled a job (changing grading) that brought us square against one of the most important issues to faculty members, and that is the control they are able to exert over students and student behavior. That control is the grade. Generally, that is an implicit kind of a control. Generally, they don't see themselves as wanting to manipulate students. They see themselves as having responsibility to judge the work of apprentices. I suppose that is not too bad a statement. But it's part of the system that students are generally paid (with grades) for providing services which are in the form of regurgitation. There are faculty who have other expectations but I find they have less interest in grades, too. So we tackled a project where we didn't have the power to effect change ourselves. We had to become a lobbying group. As such we did the best job we could. We had no votes. Of the fifty-five people on the senate, none of those people were members of our group. We could not have direct influence, we could only try to persuade. I did a follow-up, mailed survey of the members of the representative assembly to see what kind of activities and experiences were influential in the formation of their attitudes on this grading proposal. The things that were most significant were their own experiences as teachers and as students. The things that were least influential were the report that I disseminated, journal articles on the subject of grading, and so forth. The interview that we did was just slightly above the paper in influence. It seems to me that in working for change in an issue that is this central to the lives of the faculty, whether or not it is explicitly perceived as a threat, the response is certainly defensive behavior.

Overcoming Problems

Team projects can be successful only if the latent energies of members are made available for team action. A project requires a higher level of intensity of pursuit of goals than does ordinary work on the campus. Yet as mentioned earlier in this chapter, a universal problem is to find a minimum amount of time to spend working together because of member schedules. The school calendar, with its peaks of activity at examination times and lulls during vacations, makes it difficult to maintain intense involvement in a team.

Member turnover also is a serious problem. Our initial conception was formation of a more-or-less durable group. Actually, few members participated during the entire life of the study. Recruitment of new members was a continual process as students graduated, faculty went on leave or transferred, administrators took new jobs, and so on. But to solve this problem, our teams developed techniques for enlisting and maintaining new members. One gave new members the same status as old members and developed a process of deliberately bringing new members into the fold. The emotional support of being an accepted member of a team can give people the energy and strength to carry on. Since most members are volunteers, the team must be aware of the payoffs it is giving them to remain on the team. These include finding a role for each member that makes him or her feel important or giving the member a chance to expand and develop new skills. Since students often are shorter term members than are campus employees, they need faster payoffs.

One strategy to overcome the problem of team instability was to join it to the college structure. Tactics included running the team as a course in group dynamics or planned change, using team members as section discussion leaders for courses, assigning credit to students for project work, giving faculty and administrators time for the project as part of their jobs, and paying members for work such as interviewing. Yet, in spite of these devices, team membership was basically voluntary; and capturing the time of members was a continual problem. Teams that were built around common interests seemed to be more durable and effective than were those that were "representative." Such commonality of interest boosts motivation for work. Also, as noted previously, consultants have an important function in sparking interest and activity, thereby increasing team stability.

Leader-group differences often occur, usually after some time. Leaders may recruit team members to help them in projects only to find later that these members limit the leaders' freedom as they become involved and creative. The leader may then drop out of the project. Or, more dramatically, the team may discover a divergence between its aims and the leader's and force him or her out.

Power struggles are not confined to internal team affairs. They may ensue if the project overlaps the territory of other groups. As one member concluded, "Change almost always involves a redistribution of power and assets." A project team can therefore expect much opposition. Pressure is certain to be felt by the more marginal team members, such as untenured faculty. We cannot resist quoting the leader of a change team who felt that his team had little power. "Power corrupts," he said, "but lack of power is absolutely corrupting!"

We have found that teams are better able to survive in the face of conflicts with outside forces when they are cohesive as a group. Teams that are mutually supportive and in which the members understand each other can learn and grow as a result of challenges. Those which have weak internal development are likely to collapse when opposed. Teams are also aided by building skill in analyzing the forces which are in their favor and those which are opposed to their efforts so that the conflicts which arise are not surprising. Teams can devise suitable strategies for dealing with the resistances they encounter. It helps to realize that some conflict is natural even in an overall collaborative change strategy.

One resource which we thought would be helpful to overcome various problems was training grants to allow members to attend two-week NTL summer sessions dealing with campus change. Usually members attended as subgroups of a team and focused on planning for the next semester as well as on developing personal and group skills. From what we could see and from what was reported, this additional training did reinforce members' commitments to their teams. It also however posed problems of integrating the subgroups with the rest of the team while raising the level of skills available for group process work. Going to these laboratories also did not seem to contribute directly to task achievement, but they clearly influenced the style of the teams. The workshops which were provided specifically for entire teams were unequivocally viewed by members as being of great value. As one team member put it, "I feel that if we didn't have some of these workshops the team would be a lot less energetic, not as vital, maybe not even existent. So I feel that workshops were very important to us."

Working with outside consultants also helped the teams in struggling to achieve their goals. Outside people can provide very valuable assistance even if they do not spend a lot of time with the group. Their chief impact on the teams in our project was in mobilizing team energies. It is clear to us that they were highly responsible for the continuity and durability of these mainly volunteer groups. Connections to consultants validates the team's existence, objectives, and growth in the institution, according to team members. Consultant visits as well as workshops provided a discipline sustained by eagerness among team members to please the consultants. Consultants' appearances provided occasions for review of progress, reassessment of goals, and commitment. One member made this same statement more facetiously, "Whether or not consultants have expectations for your performance, it is better to believe they do!"

Consultants also, of course, bring to a team information and skill. They can provide perspective, a mirror to the group to show how it is doing; they can share the experiences of other groups and help in dealing with internal and external problems. As one member put it, "Consultants—outside, or from other parts of the campus, may stumble over things you have been avoiding." Consultant efforts were very effective in promoting a self-examining style with the aid of members who could help perform this function. We noted that the procedure of having one team act as consultants to another team during the interteam workshops also was very effective.

Some illuminating statements about the value of consultants were made at the retrieval conference:

> *Bailiff* (University of California, Davis) : It seems
> that one of the things that happened was that bringing
> the team of consultants helped the people in the Alliance

use their own resources. Somehow prior to that point they just felt impotent. They didn't get much going. So they brought in some high-powered dudes but found that they themselves had all along a lot of energy that they couldn't tap. Then they could mobilize their own resources. That was an interesting phenomenon.

Finch (University of Massachusetts): My sense is that internal change teams just have got incredible problems. They are in a low power situation; but when you get someone from the outside, legitimacy and all kinds of other things happen.

Shoffiett (Antioch College): The relationship to NTL sensitized us to some of the environmental variables. Like what was possible in the institution at that time. The consultation helped us to develop strategies that gave us resources and made it possible for us to cope. We had resources that we would not have received. The program was able to do things that it would not have been able to do with the resources that were willingly given to us . . . instead of running into the wind headlong, standing back a little and developing a coping strategy and realizing that the wind was maybe a brick wall, and finally being able to feel when the wind was a brick wall.

Conclusion

Most members found the continual tension in shifting from personal and group growth to task work to be a unique experience but one that created a time-sharing problem. Task-oriented groups found that a focus on personal and group processes slowed them down initially. The quick movement from problem statement, to goal setting, to action came to a halt for one group when it began to deal more with interpersonal issues. However, once the process became incorporated into the team's repertoire, it could move smoothly with improved participation, more learning for members, and increased commitment to team decisions. Paying attention to this wide array of events does cost time and energy, but teams that employed techniques of both individual and group development while working on a project could build enough motivation and cohesion to sustain them during periods of high frustration and low morale. As one of the team members formulated it: $E = G \times (PR^2)$, where E = energy, G = goal value, PR = personal rewards for members. Thus the energy available for work on a project equals the value of the goal or task for members, times the square of their personal rewards. If the goal has no value, there will be no energy. If personal rewards are low, much less energy will be expended than if they are even moderately high. We do not vouch for the mathematics in the formula—but its concept seems sound.

The most effective teams, we believe, focus on personal growth, team development, and campus change, but there are many difficulties in achieving this synthesis. Some teams find warmth and comfort in the group and hesitate to venture outside: sociability is easier to achieve than is campus reform! On the other hand it is easy to fall into a strict focus on the task and forget to look at how the process is going. Not only do teams vary in their focus on internal and external relations but the basis of members' attraction to the team varies; some are attracted to the groups by their interest in campus reform, some by their interest in personal relationships, and others by a desire for professional training. A mix of member motivations is obviously necessary, or at least it is unavoidable. The mixture puts a premium on maintaining a balance between task and personal needs.

A consultant strategy was to provide a high level of personal and group development sessions during the longer workshops. These experiences helped the teams to jell as cohesive units with strong, effective ties. Yet, as one member pointed out, "alternating or separating campus change efforts with personal and interpersonal activities is not the answer. They need to be worked in together. You can make the development of personal and interpersonal skills a group task." Two options are available: one is to have activities aimed specifically at team development; another is to deal with personal issues only when they arise in the course of task work.

As predicted from our earlier analysis, the teams attracted, for the most part, people who were not in the institutional main stream. They tended to be in low power positions: students, untenured faculty, staff of special programs, student affairs people, or assistant provosts in charge of innovative programs. Innovations frequently are initiated by the less powerful and are built by a process of adoption by higher levels. It also has been noted that more business innovations originate at higher levels in the organization, but more *successful* innovations originate at lower levels—because lower level innovations are screened more carefully whereas higher level ones are likely to be directed into existence. Project teams provide opportunities for initiation from persons with low official power.

We conclude that the effective use of teams as change agents on the campus has been demonstrated. However, the technology of change teams is still very rudimentary. We can describe the stages a team has to go through, some of the critical tasks it has to perform, some ways of being successful, and some ways to fail; yet our knowledge of the variables is partial. We cannot identify all of the conditions and ways of dealing with them: that makes the process of working for change unpredictable. It means there is no specific set of instructions for a team to follow; the methods need to custom-fit the situation. The ingredients for success that we suggest are in the manual, Part Two of this book.

In a sense, the product is the process. As long as we are engaged in critically examining our institutions and their impact on our lives, we can be moved to commitment and to dedicated action. We believe that is the right track and that project teams help us to stay on it. Unexamined institutions are not worth living in!

PART II

MANUAL FOR CHANGE TEAMS

In Part One we presented a wide range of crucial tasks which higher educational institutions are facing, such as countering falling enrollments, meeting financial crises, eliminating racism and sexism, reforming governance, adjusting programs to meet social and personal needs, improving teaching and learning, and making institutions humane and effective. The action-research change teams we are discussing here cannot in the short run solve problems of that magnitude; they can, however, aid in moving toward solutions by translating large issues into specific goals and by devising actions to move in desired directions.

The purpose of this manual is to help you use your group as an agent of change, whether you are a member of a group, an administrator, a student, a faculty member, or a consultant. The manual presents tips, procedures, ideas, and activities which we have found useful in our work with campus change teams.

We believe it is important to share all available skill and knowledge in this area. Educational institutions must be able to make effective changes in order to cope with the problems they face. Business as usual will not suffice. We therefore foresee an acceleration of efforts by institutions to make changes, and we assume many of these innovative attempts will involve group effort—as they have in the past. But we predict most of these groups will not be effective or contribute to the learning and satisfaction of their members. We believe this manual can help you to create more productive and more satisfying groups.

Sarason (1972) discusses the difficulties encountered in trying to build new organizations (settings). He points out that most new settings, from marriages to revolutions, do not succeed. One reason for the high rate of failure is the common assumption on the part of those entering a new venture that shared values and a high level of motivation are sufficient to produce success. In fact, creating any new setting is extremely complex and requires a wide range of skill and knowledge in addition to commitment. Sarason (1972, p. 6) says: "Beyond values, the creation of settings involves (among other things . . .) substantive knowledge, a historical stance, a realistic time perspective, vehicles of criticism, and the necessity for and the evils of leadership. The creation of settings is not an engineering or technological task. It is also not one that can be accomplished simply by having appropriate or strong motivation."

The groups we are discussing are new settings with all the needs Sarason points out: motivation, skill, and knowledge. As we see them, the core tasks for these groups are recruiting and motivating members, developing adequate group processes, linking to other parts of the system, planning for and doing work, and proceeding in a way which is self-renewing. These tasks are performed during the phases of the change process: achieving clarity about goals, building commitment and resources, and taking action. This manual deals with these aspects of change and team building. It will provide you with concepts for looking at, talking about, and understanding what is happening in a change project. We also suggest specific activities which teams can use to diagnose their condition and to take appropriate actions. We see this manual as a road map to help in determining where a group has been, where it is, and where it is going. In addition we present here ideas about things to do at wayside stops which will make the trip enjoyable and successful.

The manual is organized as follows: Section I looks at various ways of starting teams and the implications of these methods. Sections II through VI explore the various capabilities which teams need. The issues relating to the use of consultants or doing without them are presented in Section VII. Section VIII presents some ideas and techniques for action-oriented research. A number of team development activities are described in Section IX.

I

How Teams Get Started

Certain clues often indicate that a change team can be useful. Persistent institutional problems may require joint attention from several units of the college. People may be interested in creating programs involving several parts of the organization. Long-range unsettled issues may need continuity of effort and attention. An individual or a subgroup may want to produce a change which impinges on others' areas of control. Interest in self-study by the institution or a subunit may be expressed. You may feel a need for better use of data in decision-making. You may desire to reach collaborative decisions that members of the institution will feel they made. You may wish to combine work on institutional issues with personal and professional development. Problems or programs with which teams have worked range from creating a new student-run, volunteer counseling service and reforming the undergraduate psychology program of a university to attempting to alter a traditional letter grading system, improving student services in a variety of areas, starting a campus radio station, and training students, faculty and staff in human relations, organizational development, and planned-change skills.

Change teams can begin in several ways. Three common

approaches to getting such groups started are spontaneous joining together of persons with a common interest, establishment by a department or other unit, and creation by administrators of the institution. These categories are not mutually exclusive: A group may start out as a self-generated advocacy group and then be adopted by the formal system; or a team may simultaneously be established by a department and be sanctioned by the institution at large. These various ways of starting teams have important implications.

Self-appointed groups. A change team can start as an informal group which wants to initiate an innovation and which has as its main purpose bringing about a change in some aspect of the environment outside of itself. In one such case, an administrator who wanted to provide alternatives to the traditional counseling system gathered a self-selected group of interested faculty and students together. This group eventually created a new type of counseling center. The group then moved on to work on other tasks, and in time it became an official part of the organization. This start-up process differed from having the counseling service create a group to improve its own practices or having a team appointed by the president to work on the issue of counseling.

The self-appointed group has maximum freedom to select its goals and strategies. It can tap the energy of those who wish to champion a cause, and it can acquire members with interest and commitment. But early and crucial tasks for the self-initiated group include establishing legitimacy, getting resources (such as time for members to work on the project, money, and space), and countering suspicion by those in authority. After all, the creation of a self-appointed change group implies criticism of the institution. Moreover, a self-appointed group generally has difficulty operating in a genuinely collaborative style with the bureaucracy. Developing a base of support and interest typically requires the team to adopt an advocacy stance and press its "cause" against existing policies, instead of serving as a facilitator, data gatherer, resource, and catalyst. Such a stance does not preclude collaboration with those affected by the change, but it may make it difficult.

Groups set-up by an organizational unit. A team can be established by a department, a school, or some other unit that wishes to change itself. The team becomes a facilitator of improvement of the unit because it is an integral part of the unit. For example, a group of students and faculty was given the responsibility by a department of psychology to gather data about the department program and help generate desirable changes in it. The group collected and organized extensive information from graduates, employers, students, and faculty. They engaged students and faculty in drawing conclusions from the data and then helped to generate participation among members of the department in creating a number of changes.

This way of beginning provides ideal opportunities for using an action-research approach which involves data collection, diagnosis, action, and evaluation. There are built-in connections between the team and others. The team has an excellent opportunity to become accepted as a helper and a resource, for it is not easy to define such a team as an outside agitator. Commitment tends to be high because the team is working on issues of direct concern to members.

The major task in this case is to avoid being seen as a group with values and goals different from those of the rest of the department. The team needs to define itself as a distinct group to develop and function, but its connections with the rest of the unit need to be kept well oiled to minimize separation and "we-they" interactions.

Groups created by the administration. Officials of a college may create a change group to deal with a particular problem or to generate innovation. This team becomes to a considerable extent a servant of the institution, although it may achieve considerable independence. In one case, the administration of a university wanted more student involvement in making decisions in academic departments. At the initiative of several key administrators, a team of students, faculty members, and administrators was created to work toward that goal. They used an action-research approach to support and evaluate departmental student advisory committees. The team was a key factor in the success of that program and continued to be supported by top administrators.

The main strength of this model is its built-in link with power. Thus the issues of legitimacy and acquisition of resources (faculty time, for instance) are moderated. The group has a mandate for action and a charge that defines its role. Its establishment helps administrators to gain collaboration in change efforts—but they must be willing to give the team enough freedom for it to mature and achieve potency.

Key tasks are building workable links between the team and others in the institution. The group tends to be viewed as a tool of the "establishment"—a perception which often provokes suspicion, hostility, and resistance. Also, since the task is assigned, members may not feel a sense of personal commitment to it. You may find much work needed to define goals which the team feels it "owns." (As a case in point, the team mentioned above never fully felt ownership of the group goals, which proved to be a problem throughout its several years of existence.)

II

Recruiting and Motivating Members

The membership of the group certainly will affect the building of a team which works well together and has connections, abilities, and self-renewal potential. Your team should be composed of an array of persons who can help its performance. You should look periodically to see whether changes in composition of the team, its goals, or the surrounding environment require membership adjustments.

Your overall task is to build a team with sufficient strength to have a reasonable chance of success. Either modify the goal or modify the team if progress is not being achieved. An unsuccessful team becomes frustrated and tends to resist future participation in campus change efforts. Some risk is involved in any change venture, but success can be achieved by trying to make the potency of the team consonant with its objectives. You must note, however, that bureaucratic status is not synonymous with potency as a team member.

Member Motivations

Understanding and supporting the motivations of the individual are important in building team membership. In working with campus change teams, we have explored such questions as: What does the member hope to gain personally? What motivates her or him to put a significant amount of time and energy into the team? What are the most attractive features of the team activity? What are the forces that influence people to continue or to discontinue membership in the team? We found these answers on the positive side: joining an exciting and worthwhile project, increasing involvement and influence on campus, learning new skills in group dynamics and planned change, changing conditions that have been personally unsatisfying, exploring and extending one's own skills and abilities, learning more about oneself, working with outside consultants and participating in training activities, spending time with friends or valued colleagues or making new friends, and associating with faculty (or students) in a peer–colleague–co-worker relationship.

Different members seek and achieve different satisfactions. Frequently members comment that they continue with the team primarily because they enjoy associations with members and because they learn from team experiences. For most members, however, interest in working on the task is combined with a desire for personal growth or rewarding relationships. In order to maintain motivation, your team will need both satisfactions. You should explore explicitly and openly members' motivations and whether their needs are being met. All our teams have periodically engaged in extensive discussion in which each member reports on why he is a member, what he wants to gain, and what he wants to work on in the next few months. Such sessions can be coupled nicely to a contracting session, in which members build agreements with each other about how they wish to relate. It is essential for you to legitimize the team's serving as a resource for its members as well as working toward promoting outside change.

Typical Problems

Common difficulties in the area of membership and motivation are discussed in the following paragraphs.

If your team develops into a tight in-group, it may have difficulty attracting or accepting new members. Many of our teams experienced this feeling during the first year or so. For example, one group which had become close was reluctant to recruit new members, although attrition was wearing down the team. Members were beginning to be perceived as elitist and were putting most of their energy into group maintenance. The team became more effective after it finally invited new members in and designed a good way of integrating them. The new members were valued for their energy and new ideas.

Failure to recruit high-status teaching faculty who are willing to devote sufficient time to the team is a common shortcoming— but not a disaster.

Failure to have fun together is a serious shortcoming in a volunteer group. We do not mean fun in the sense only of amusement but also of gaining satisfaction from relationships and from learning. Team members report that they enjoy opportunities to increase their self-awareness, to learn about group process, and to learn about social change. It also helps to devote some meeting time to social activities, to bring in exciting consultants, to have workshops in pleasant places, and to develop satisfying interpersonal relationships. Especially important is the legitimization of having a good time as a part of the group maintenance process instead of viewing it as mere flight from work.

Unrealistic expectations of members about the amount or pace of change create problems. It is critical that you point out the complexity of achieving even apparently simple changes in organizations without emphasizing the difficulties to the point of discouragement. Realism is helpful, cynicism is not.

Failure to maintain reasonably stable membership or failure to plan ahead for replacing departing members in an orderly and timely way causes severe difficulties. It is particularly important in the spring to recruit for replacement of members who will not be returning in the fall. (One team discovered in the summer that it would have only one on-going member in the fall. The team died.)

Not enabling each member to make a significant contribution to the team results in low commitment. You should see to it that each member has a significant part to play compatible with his time, energy, other commitments, and skills. Functions tend to centralize in a few persons, leaving the rest of the group as marginally involved spectators. That pattern is discouraging.

Energy will not be maintained unless your team can perceive its successes. Establish a pattern of pointing out how your team is moving toward its goals. Achievements should be noted on the change task and also in the learning and satisfaction of members.

Not allowing for variations in time and interest among members may be a problem. Conflicts frequently arise between members with high investment and those with lower apparent investment. We have found, however, that considerable variation in participation can be tolerated cheerfully if the differences and the reasons for them are openly explored.

Guidelines

Guidelines for recruiting, maintaining membership, and motivating are as follows:

The skills that your team needs to acquire depend on the nature of the change project, the institutional dynamics, the history of related efforts, how the team is linked to other parts of the college, and the need for adequate procedures within the group. These factors need to be taken into account in recruiting.

Your team can build the skills it needs by recruitment or by training current members. The process of recruiting members should be mutual, however. Give the potential member a chance to assess the satisfying aspects of membership and the team a chance to assess the candidate's skill and commitment. Realistic orientation for new members also is important and is a recurring need.

You should be aware of the importance of maintaining the interest of team members because for volunteers intrinsic rewards are crucial as there usually are no extrinsic rewards.

You should remember that the problem of maintaining membership is chronic: student generations pass quickly and faculty move, retire, and go on leaves.

A balance of research, direct action opportunities, and personal growth experiences helps to sustain motivation.

Each member needs a significant role to play that matches his or her time and energy.

Your team needs a process to convey to members a sense of progress toward the goals.

Your team should recognize and deal openly with the pressures members feel from competing demands and conflicting loyalties.

It is more important for your team to be cohesive and energetic than for it to be representative.

III

Selecting Change Goals

Unlike the typical campus committee, your change team may begin with only a general definition of a goal. ("To reduce non-productive student stress" was the goal that brought one of our teams together. The group then moved on to try to reform the grading system.) Your team may initially have a closely defined objective, but it must still determine its own operational goals. It must also move from a problem statement, such as "there are not enough women faculty members," to a goal statement, such as "we want to double the number of women professors within two years." Goal setting is a universal and recurring process for teams and must be based on: a mutual agreement and understanding among team members; available resources and energy; an ability to effect changes in a reasonable time period; and an assessment of potential relationships with its clients.

Process

Selection or definition of the goal is your team's most critical act. It controls to a considerable degree the future course of the team. Table 1 will help you to select a goal and can be used as follows:

Table 1.

GOAL SELECTION MATRIX

Change Units	*Goal Selection Factors*				
	Understanding	Commitment	Power	Time Perspective	Amount and Kind of Change
Individual Team Members					
Team					
Specific Clientele					
Larger Organization					

Your team can start with a short discussion of the Goal Selection Matrix. Then it should discuss its goal and place a mark in each cell where there are perceived problems. For instance, if the team does not agree on the desired degree of "radicalness" which the goal should reflect, a mark should be placed in the second row "Team" and the last column "Amount and Kind of Change." Or if members cannot state to each other's satisfaction what the goal is, place a check in the "Individual Team Members Understanding" box. The problem points can be identified by scanning to see where the marks are. The group can then develop priorities for the issues which are most pressing, list causes of the problems, and plan how to deal with them.

Note that highly innovative goals need especially serious consideration, for the more radical the change, the greater the risk of failure and also the greater the amount of institutional criticism to be expected.

Factors and Problems

Understanding goal. The problem area your team is concerned about leads it to formulate a change goal—a future state free of some existing problems. Team members need to be able to state clearly and convincingly what that future state would be, why change is needed, and "where we ought to be." Your team needs to be sure that its own members and other relevant members of the organization are aware of the goal and understand it clearly.

Common difficulties related to understanding the goal are:

(1) Inability of the group to make a clear, concise statement, in one sentence, of what it is doing; for example, "our team is trying to change the grading system from conventional letter grades to a more educationally useful method of evaluation."

(2) Lack of understanding of the relationship between gathering data and producing change. For action research, you should ask how the answers to questions might be used in creating action steps before you make the inquiry.

(3) Too quickly assuming there is a shared understanding of the goal and possibly glossing over differences which will plague you later. For instance, experimental college faculties which join each other on the basis of a shared desire for innovation may not explore their values far enough. They may discover that one person sees innovation as great books programs and the other sees it as universal encounter groups.

Commitment to goal. Commitment refers to the level of enthusiasm and the amount of energy that can be mobilized in support of the goal. The test, of course, is whether you are willing to divert time and energy from pursuit of other goals to pursuit of this one. Commitment enables the team to move from awareness of the problem to working toward the goal. Open exploration and testing of members' own desires is a good start toward building a common commitment. You should highlight similarities and commonalities as well as differences. Groups often wrangle over small differences while overlooking large commonalities which can provide a framework for resolving disagreements.

Common difficulties related to commitment to the goal are:

(1) Not involving the object of the change effort in formulating the goal statement, for it can resist the change. (If you want to start a faculty development program, it is a good idea to ask the faculty what needs they sense and what training they might like before defining your program goals.) Do not build goals which

merely flow from your own desires and are unrelated to the experience of the target of change.

(2) Not choosing a goal grand enough to be exciting and specific enough to be achievable. Teams need both a vision and a reachable objective. Establishment of subobjectives within a broad goal helps to resolve this problem.

(3) Teams accept goals suggested by influential persons without adequately testing the real commitment of all members to those objectives. (One team accepted a goal defined by an exiting dean who was a member of the group. None of the other members was particularly excited about the task but they liked working with the dean. Unfortunately, he left the school and the team then had low energy for completing the project. Another team which in effect had its goal assigned by the university administration never succeeded in generating full commitment to working toward that goal.)

Power. Power is the ability to overcome resistance to change. Potential power sources are: coercion, the support of allied groups, appealing to value systems, presenting information, the desire for self- and organizational improvement, and providing economic rewards. The team must be able to use some of these levers in order to generate movement toward the goal. (Coercion is not a power source which is appropriate to use in a collaborative change process but it is basic to some other change models.)

You should capitalize on the available power because: teams that feel potent are more active and members are more involved; they are less likely to rehash decisions which have been made; they achieve better follow-through on decisions; they are likely to have better group processes with less dysfunctional subgrouping and better quality of interaction; and in a word, a sense of being able to produce movement in the direction it wants to go adds "tone" to your group. (An action-research team was able to convert its work on data collection and action planning into gaining money to start a new program of clinical training for students. That program was precisely in line with their goals. The group acquired a real sense of power and achieved some significant innovations.)

Common difficulties in goal setting relating to power are:

(1) Kind and amount of power potentially available to the team which is inappropriate to achievement of the goals. (If you

wish to use a typical organizational development model, for instance, you must have influence with the formal power figures in the institution. If you do not have that kind of power, you should consider changing your goal to accommodate to one of an advocacy group. Then you can use common interests among members of the institution to build power for change.)

(2) Failure to identify interests, motivations, and values within other parts of the institution which will support your goals. A corollary of this problem is failure to recognize lack of support of influential on-campus interest groups or individuals. (A team which was trying to start an alternative counseling service for students did not sufficiently test the degree of support from student affairs officers. These persons later tried to block opening the center. A great deal of effort was required to counteract that inhibiting influence.)

(3) Failure to include in goal setting the possible support of off campus groups which are linked to the campus and could help with the project. (The team mentioned above established its goal as developing a student-run help center which would include drug counseling. This goal was set in part because the team defined its objectives in a way to make it possible to receive a grant from the state.)

(4) Failure to link goals to the rewards which your team can offer its members. These rewards generally are intrinsic: learning, affiliation, and satisfaction. If you keep those rewards in mind, you will realize it is unrealistic to set goals that will require large amounts of members' time on a continuous basis.

Time perspectives. Goals must be realistic in relation to a specific time framework—which can be short-range, intermediate, or long-range. You may have all three time frames simultaneously by identifying short-range objectives which are linked to longer range objectives. We strongly urge establishing such subgoals. (For instance, getting a questionnaire analyzed, a workshop organized, or a series of interviews completed should be recognized as goal achievements even though the larger mission remains incomplete.) With a "ladder" of goals, team members can maintain interest in an important venture by being able to mark off specific progress.

Common difficulties in goal setting relating to time perspective are:

(1) Unrealistic expectations about the rate of change generates frustration for students who want to see changes made within their own tenure. You should help students and others to see the complexity of change so they are not led to expect speedy, large-scale achievements. (A primarily student group undertook to improve instruction at its college. Members became discouraged after two years with the pace of change, among other things, and discontinued the group.) You can help keep that kind of effort going by making members realize that most teams need about three years to achieve a really significant impact, and by helping them to note the progress they have made.

(2) Differences in feelings about the appropriate rate of change among various groups in the college. (An administrator at one institution where we were starting a team recommended two years of data collection and analysis followed by tentative action steps in the third year, and vigorous action in the fourth year. Students, as well as others, found those time goals unappealing and attempted to greatly speed up the process.)

(3) Failing to divide the tasks to be accomplished into successive time periods and keeping track of progress to provide a sense of movement. (A group which wanted to organize a network of campus change agents set this goal sequence: getting a proposal for funding to the university, getting the money, hiring consultants, getting support from departments, and organizing a large workshop to extend membership. These steps were spread over a six-month period and the group's success at accomplishing each one was highly energizing.)

(4) Failing to make goals fit the school calendar. (One group set long-term goals in May and then departed for the summer. When they returned in the fall, there were several membership changes and old members had new perspectives. The entire goal setting process had to be repeated. The May goals would better have been focused on how to get started in the fall and how to use the summer productively.)

(5) Failing to understand that goals do not remain static but must be reviewed and revised frequently. There is a common expectation that goals are set at one time and then diagnosis, action, and evaluation follow. You should realize, however, that data

collection and action steps influence members' perceptions, requiring reconsideration and modification of goals. Changing circumstances also require goal revision. (A team at a workship in June set a goal and a series of subgoals for the following year. A strike at the beginning of the school year radically changed the setting in which they were to work. The team did not readjust its goals quickly enough and spent several debilitating months working toward out-of-date objectives.)

Amount and kind of change. Changes may be skin pinches or jugular-cuts. Change can aim at increasing an organization's ability to accommodate to external and internal stress, or change can attempt to transcend current arrangements and revamp the structures. If your group is employing the collaborative, action-research mode, it is more likely to be working on transformation than on radical reform—but teams often differ about how radical a change should be. (For instance, a project team working on involving students in decision-making was periodically plagued by differences of opinion on whether it should stick to the task of making student advisory committees more effective or whether it should push for a really fundamental shift of power to students.)

Common difficulties in goal setting relating to the amount and type of change are:

(1) Failing to consider the impact of the goal on all of the social units involved. (A team which established a goal of improving student services and generating more student leadership did not anticipate the impact of these goals on the established student government. Considerable hostility resulted and took many months to resolve.) When setting goals, you should try to be aware of the potential impact on all units affected.

(2) Failing to make the degree and type of change being contemplated appropriate to the resources of the group. (A team composed primarily of students and student affairs people undertook to change a university grading system. This was a large-scale core issue to which members had very few institutional connections. The group also had little money, time, staff assistance, or consulting support in view of the magnitude of their goal. Little progress was made toward that goal, although in some respects the team was a success.)

(3) Losing the views of persons who aim at either ultrastability or radical transformation because they are unlikely to join your team or are uncomfortable when they are there. If groups are too heterogenous, they spend too much time in mediating member differences. To generate drive, a team does well to have a high level of commonality. However, in setting goals, you should take into account the reactions of those persons with different values. To keep in touch, members can be assigned to interview persons with known differences and report to the rest of the team those person's reactions.

(4) Failing to build connections between your group's goals and other campus issues which could generate a positive chain reaction. Teams often become too isolated and inbred. The goals your team choose should include statements about linking with other related efforts on the campus.

IV

Building a Team

A collection of individuals becomes a team when they develop ways of thinking, feeling, and working together. Team unity depends on the capacity of members to mesh their ideas, motives, and abilities; so to build unity, some attention must focus on internal development. This process, however, in the long-run, generates increased energy to devote to the external task. A unified team is able to develop a goal, commit itself to achieving it, and work together to reach it. You should recognize and understand these three aspects of team development if your group is to operate effectively.

The developmental process for groups is rather complex; it takes time to build a mature, well-functioning group. It helps in working with teams to have a way of thinking about group developmental flow. One perspective which we find useful is provided by Schutz (1958) in his Fundamental Interpersonal Response Orientation (FIRO) theory. He sees group development as going through three phases: inclusion, control, and affection. Inclusion is the key issue during the initial phase of group life, when the members are concerned with who is in and who is out of the group, the meaning of membership, the history of the group, and the feelings of other persons who may want to enter or leave the group. Control issues tend to dominate the next phase of group development with concerns about dominance, authority and power, and influence on decision-making and action. In the third phase, issues of intimacy tend to come to the fore with group members focusing on questions of how close, expressive, trusting, and confiding they want to be. (All these issues are present throughout group life; it is relative emphasis during any one phase that is being described here.)

A group tends to function well to the degree that it has dealt with all these issues in some depth and is capable of coming back to them for further explorations as the situation dictates. The emotional component of each of the three phases makes it important to allow sufficient time for the development of the group and to pay attention to difficulties the group may have in dealing well with each area. We present below ways of addressing these central issues to facilitate the maturing of the group.

A related view of the developmental process in groups is illustrated by the Menninger morale curve, based on observations of the Peace Corps training groups staffed by the Menninger Foundation. In general, they found that groups started out with rather high morale, which peaked soon after the training had begun. Morale then dopped dramatically as evidenced by high conflict, boredom, desire to withdraw, and criticism of many aspects of the program and the surroundings. The morale next tended to go back up until it peaked and started to decline either just prior to or soon after departure. This morale curve is related to four major crisis points in the life of a group: entrance, involvement, acceptance, and separation. Upon arrival, members tend to have somewhat unrealistic expectations which elevate their morale. When people get engaged with each other, however, the realities of the situation become apparent—including interpersonal tensions and requirements for work which may not be totally appealing. As members learn to accept each other, develop strong bonds, and accept the realities of the common work to be done, morale goes back up. It dips again around the end of the group when members begin to feel the pain of separating from each other. These crises parallel the central issues identified by Schutz and add the morale dimension.

Table 2 is a tool for diagnosing the developmental state of

a team and to plan appropriate activities. It is based on the following assumptions about team needs:

(1) Achieving goal clarity requires that team members have a high degree of communication and understanding of one another's thoughts, feelings, interests, and values; ways of checking their assumptions and understandings with each other; and a common focus of interest.

(2) Acquiring goal commitment requires that team members express and adjust their individual goals to form a group goal; be concerned with the personal needs of other members; use the creative and analytic skills of all members; apply enthusiasm and energy, sometimes even vehemently and impatiently, to team work; and feel their own needs are being met by working toward the goal.

(3) Building skills in working as a team requires identifying functions which need to be performed and developing roles to cover them; having effective and flexible procedures which focus on solving problems rather than on maintaining members' statuses in the group; building and following agendas; assessing progress on the path toward the goal; observing team procedures and correcting inadequacies; and providing explicit training in group process and task-related skills.

One way of using this table is for your team to discuss each stage in the left-hand column. For any stage which appears to be problematical, look at the forces which are impinging on the team. For instance, you may determine that the goal is understood, but your team is not fully committed to it because it has adopted the goal of a dominant member without building others' interests in it. Dealing with that issue requires a climate in which the group can confront both the sponsor of the goal and the members who did not express their needs. Your team will need to build interpersonal supports to open up the issues. Then you should make sure each member will feel rewarded by working toward the goal which is finally set.

We now discuss the key problems which impede a group from developing into an effective team.

Inadequate interpersonal communication. To facilitate and ease interpersonal communications, train your team in the skills of describing others' behavior, describing one's own feelings, and

Table 2.
Assessing Developmental Needs of a Team

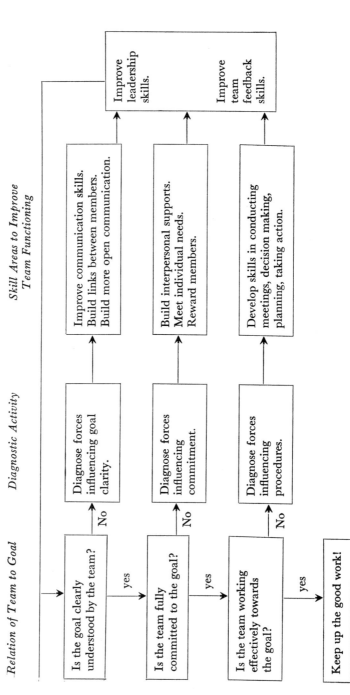

Relation of Team to Goal	Diagnostic Activity	Skill Areas to Improve Team Functioning

Is the goal clearly understood by the team? — No → Diagnose forces influencing goal clarity. → Improve communication skills. Build links between members. Build more open communication. → Improve leadership skills.

yes ↓

Is the team fully committed to the goal? — No → Diagnose forces influencing commitment. → Build interpersonal supports. Meet individual needs. Reward members.

yes ↓

Is the team working effectively towards the goal? — No → Diagnose forces influencing procedures. → Develop skills in conducting meetings, decision making, planning, taking action. → Improve team feedback skills.

yes ↓

Keep up the good work!

checking one's perceptions of others' feelings and ideas. For your group to increase its awareness, ideas and feelings must be shared, especially among persons who differ from one another. To work productively together, a team needs to identify and overcome gaps in information and attitudes. You should not begrudge time devoted to building these communication skills. You may find it helpful to occasionally take meeting time to ask a person how he or she is feeling about membership in the team.

Most team members talk easily about task issues and fairly easily about interpersonal relationships, but with difficulty about their individual needs. Each team develops norms about how direct and open members should be with one another. These norms range from open and accepting to closed and defensive. Innovation and creativity are aided by open, accepting climates in which there is freedom to explore ideas and feelings. You should therefore build norms that support increased openness in both personal and task areas. (We have seen cases where only personal commitment and loyalty to each other have kept a group together during a low period.) Regardless of one's interest in a task, loyalty to another person is much more binding.

Groups have difficulty in shifting a climate of behavior once it is established. They tend to find a preferred mode and stay there in spite of its disadvantages. Usually groups cling unswervingly to strict work, but sometimes they become fixated on concern for interpersonal relations or individual needs and never get to an external task. The ideal is for your group to develop the ability to move smoothly back and forth between task work, examining itself, and building solid interpersonal relations. One way of facilitating that development is to give explicit responsibility to different team members for monitoring task achievement and attending to group maintenance needs. Then make sure they provide space on meeting agendas for consideration of how the team is doing.

Fragile links between members. You will find that building group unity is a continuous task. Difficulties in maintaining closeness are caused by gaps in time between meetings, lulls during vacations, people missing meetings, work being done in subgroups, subgrouping itself, having only representatives attend special meetings or workshops, and old members leaving and new ones arriving.

Keeping members hooked together takes specific attention, planning, and work. Some ways of working at the problem of lack of group unity are holding special meetings for subgroup sharing of progress, planning occasional day-long or afternoon and evening meetings, planning ahead for recruitment and presentation of new members, and going to off-campus workshops.

Low participation. After developing communication skills and building group unity, the next step is to develop norms of high involvement and participation in team activities. Participation in problem-solving increases member interest and responsibility. Frequent causes for low participation are failure to make use of the differing abilities of members; conflict between powerful members (which causes others to withdraw); unclarity about the team goal; presence of high-status members who dominate decision-making; lack of participation by highly skilled members when they do not feel sufficiently rewarded; fear of losing valued friends who disagree with the team goal; and fear of being punished by the administration.

Insufficient rewards. Rewards from membership in a volunteer action-research change team are usually intrinsic. Members are rewarded by associating with people they enjoy, working on a task they think is important, learning valued skills, being supported and encouraged by other members, and having their achievement recognized by other groups or individuals. Extrinsic rewards—academic credit, pay, or having work on the team counted as part of one's job—should be built in where possible. Such benefits from membership help members make more of their time available to the team.

However, you will find that problems may arise in this area of insufficient awards because unresolved status differences or interpersonal conflicts reduce the affiliation rewards from participation; the campus generally is indifferent or nonsupportive of the project; member loyalty to outside groups which do not support the project creates conflict; inadequate task accomplishment reduces satisfaction; or persons in influential positions outside the team do not recognize or value its achievements.

Your team should be aware of these potential problems. As with other group process issues, a period in which the group looks directly at the payoffs for membership and how people feel about them is a good occasional activity. (The University of Puerto Rico team, for instance, uses at least two meetings a year to look at what members want from membership and whether they are getting it.)

Poor group processes. The experience of working together produces a variety of tension-laden encounters. Each of your team members must develop sufficient emotional muscle to operate in settings where tension is high. Your team must develop procedures for setting the agenda, guiding discussion, and reaching decisions which enhance its ability to deal with conflict fruitfully while also progressing on its task. Throughout these processes, your team must be ready and able to deal with interpersonal relationships or individual needs when they block progress or present problems. In a task group, interpersonal problems need to be worked out only when they are relevant to the functioning of the group. (These groups differ from a sensitivity training group, in which the only purpose is the growth of its members. But they also do not operate like the conventional task-oriented committee. Thus maintaining a balance between group maintenance and task focus can be a problem.) You can see in the University of Utah case (Chapter Five) the consequences of confusion over this issue. What you need is a way of monitoring the group so that problems of inbalance or unmet needs can be brought up and dealt with successfully. Here are some common difficulties in the group process area, with tips about dealing with them:

(1) Failure to find enough time for meetings to enable members to be together to develop relationships and work on the task. We recommend fewer but longer meetings, which are often easier for people to arrange than are frequent, short meetings.

(2) Failure to develop clear agendas or procedures. For a useful agenda-building procedure, list on large sheets of paper or a blackboard items which members want considered. The items to be worked on can then be selected from all the issues listed, and the time allotted. As issues are finished, they can be checked off to tally progress.

(3) Moving from problem to solution without going through a systematic problem-solving process. There are many solutions running around looking for problems. Unfortunately, they often get hooked up with the wrong ones. We recommend this problem-

solving sequence: data collecting, diagnosis, examining alternatives, selecting and trying a course of action, and evaluating the outcome.

(4) Getting locked into traditional group procedures and member roles. Groups do not have to be hierarchical and bureaucratic, as the University of Massachusetts case points out. Try starting with a list of functions which need doing and cluster them into roles instead of doing it the other way around.

(5) Unwillingness or inability to deal with emotional issues. Change is not a rational process only; personal values and anxieties are involved also. All our teams which have lasted have been high in both confrontation and caring about each other. Your team may need to build these qualities.

(6) Inadequate leadership skills. Many leadership behaviors are required in a good group. Some are setting agendas, producing ideas, helping people to enjoy the meeting, resolving conflicts, providing personal support, and solving problems. It is usually a mistake to expect one person to perform all leadership functions. (The program at Buffalo State College, early in its life, was strongly centered on one person. Even so, it succeeded in spreading around the leadership functions to a considerable degree, which was energizing for the team.) But you should not let a misapplied egalitarian ethic inhibit zealots from pouring in energy. To build a democratic group, you do not have to make everyone the same.

(7) Other difficulties we have found are low-status members who hesitate to assume leadership; perceiving leadership as applying only to the task area; and overdependence on one or two members. You can spot these difficulties if they occur and can then move toward solving them through the group.

Insufficient feedback skills. Your team needs the ability to look at its own processes, diagnose what is happening, and use these insights to improve team functioning. Teams need continuous self-correction for which feedback is essential. There are five basic parts to an effective feedback procedure: collecting information, reporting the information to the team, making diagnoses, deciding on a course of action, and carrying out the action. Problems frequently arise, however, because not enough time is allowed for review and feedback at team meetings; responsibility for data collection and feedback is not built into the group; feedback takes time and energy from other activities which are perceived as more pressing, so it is not done; feedback arouses frustration if overdone; no design for data collection is included in agendas for team meetings; feedback is reported in a way which is perceived by some members as punitive; and problem solutions are initiated before data collection and reporting are complete.

There are several ways of ameliorating feedback problems. You may specify process observers and give them time to report their observations. You can have members fill out a short questionnaire near the end of a meeting, then tally and report the results to the total group. We suggest asking questions such as: Did you feel listened to? Did you feel influential? Did you feel supported? Were the group's resources well used? Did you enjoy the meeting? It is usually best if the answers can be discussed during the same meeting. Sometimes it is useful to start a meeting with a review of the previous session. We have also found it useful to have members and relevant other persons involved in the project to complete periodically a long questionnaire about the team and the project. These results should be reported and discussed as quickly as possible. Consultant feedback is another aid. Videotaping meetings and playing back portions of the tape are also excellent feedback mechanisms. Interviewing persons outside the group also can produce useful information to be shared with the group.

V

Working for Change

Control of the future in significant ways requires the mobilization of knowledge, resources, and power. The process of effective change, especially the introduction of an increased capability for self-change, is greatest when your team works collaboratively with the client group in identifying and mobilizing these resources. The steps in the process which we shall discuss are: clarifying and developing the roles of the change team and the client, assessing the change team's potential for helping, assessing the client's change potential, developing the goal, and developing plans and resources.

It is essential to clearly identify the client for each change effort—those persons or groups which would benefit from achievement of your team's goal. For an action-research team, the client and the change target often are the same. That is, if you are trying to improve instruction, the faculty would be a client because the team's resources would be used to aid them. The faculty would also be the primary change target because it is largely their behavior you are trying to modify. In a sense, too, the students are clients because their needs are being served. A different approach might define the administration as the client if it sponsored the team. The answer to the question "who is the client?" is not always simple. It deserves careful consideration to avoid ambiguity.

The client may be established by the process of creating a team. For instance, a department of psychology established a change team to generate reform of its own curriculum, making the department itself the client. Or, a group decided to create a woman's center so it selected women on campus as its client. In another case, a team was asked by the director of a university health program to help with staff development; that staff became the team's client. (A team may have more than one client, of course.) Often the client group is well-defined and obvious. But sometimes, however, the team must choose its client. Such choices have important implications for the team as is illustrated by the Lesley College case in Chapter Five. Change teams may find it necessary to develop enough interest to create a client group composed of people concerned about the problem on which the team wishes to work. For example, a team wishing to change a university's grading system surveyed and publicized student attitudes about grading, studied and disseminated the results of other research, and held open meetings to discuss the subject.

There are three alternative styles which a change agent team can adopt in its work with a client. These approaches in practice are often mixed, but the "pure" styles are described below.

Problem definer and solution giver. A change agent can view the client as a target to be changed: collecting information, developing a sense of needs, formulating change objectives, and creating strategies for moving the client in desired directions. This style establishes the change agent in the role of an expert (and, perhaps, a manipulator). This approach is frequently employed by college administrators. Its disadvantages are those which derive from lack of involvement, which have previously been discussed in Section III.

Data collector-feedback agent. The change-agent team can collect information about the client, organize it, and report it to the client. The data produces a mirror enabling the client to examine its own state. The process of study and feedback enables participants to perceive their shared goals and dissatisfactions. Ideally, a process of change will be set in motion. This is the approach often used with data collection techniques such as the Institutional Goals Inventory (developed by Educational Testing Service, Princeton, N.J.).

Process helper. The change agent team can help the client in all planned change steps: goal-setting, data collection, diagnosis, planning action, taking action, and evaluation. The process-oriented team helps to move the client through these steps. The University of Puerto Rico case nicely illustrates this style.

Your group can look at its skills, time, relation to the client, and the expectations of the client, and decide which of the three approaches would be preferable. Or you can look at the way your team is performing and change its procedures, if necessary, to conform to the style you prefer.

The capabilities and resources needed by the change team will depend on which change style it selects. Generally, four kinds of expertise are necessary: data collection, communication, mobilizing resources, and exercising influence. The "problem definer and solution giver" needs data collection and communication skills, as does the "data collector-feedback agent." The "process helper" needs all four capabilities. It is important for your team to have a clear view of its present and potential capacities in these areas. Your team's style, its capabilities, the client's needs, and the change task must be fitted together.

The client's change potential includes readiness and capability for change. These depend on the client's awareness of problems, ideas about how to change, ability to mobilize support for change, and available mechanisms for implementing change.

A good starting point for the change team is to look at the factors that limit members of the client group from sensing and sharing a common definition of problems. Building awareness is the first step in all collaborative change efforts. Pluralistic ignorance is a great inhibitor of change and exists when everyone assumes that no one else is aware of or concerned about his problem. Group solidarity and motivation occurs when members recognize similarities of desires. Some devices your team can use for building awareness and shared perceptions are: administer questionnaires and then feed back results in discussion groups; interview members of the group, feed back and discuss results; or conduct a problem identification discussion. If the group is large, you can conduct several small group discussions and share the results in a large meeting.

Goal development moves from a description of the present state of affairs to an imagined future state which is realistic and feasible as well as more satisfactory and productive. The goal development process aims at unfreezing people's present attitudes and behavior, such as by asking them to look at discrepancies between the way things are and the way they would like them to be. This process is discussed in detail in Section III. The point to note here is that people tend to be more open to change when they are *involved* in the goal-setting process.

An innovation is a vehicle intended to move a situation from its present state to your change goal. Developing a change plan that is clear and acceptable to the client is one of the most important aspects of innovation. Then attention, time, money, and effort must be allocated in order to realize the plan. This process is aided by: specifying subgoals, assigning dates for achieving them, listing persons who will work on them, indicating the key person who will be involved, identifying resources which will be needed by each subgroup, and agreeing on a way of monitoring and sharing progress with the whole team.

Putting planning information on large sheets of paper more or less in the following form (Table 3) is a good technique for you to follow.

An important part of your planning will be to note the changes that team members and others will need to go through to accomplish the task. Table 4 presents schematically the steps in a successful individual change process; groups go through the same process. It is helpful to keep these stages in mind when you are planing the work of your team.

These activities are needed to develop plans for change:

(1) *Locate or invent alternative solutions* by: brainstorming with persons concerned with the problem; finding out what others have done to solve similar problems; interviewing members of the client group and others to gain their ideas; consulting experts in the field; observing examples in other settings; organizing discussions for members of client group and others.

(2) *Decide which alternative to try out.* You may consider: concrete evidence that leads to the belief that the solution will work in this setting; adaptations necessary in order to fit the innovation to this setting; costs and benefits of each alternative; and examination of the forces favoring a new alternative and the forces resisting it.

Table 3.

Tasks	Workers	Completion Date	Action Steps
Prepare handbook	*Joan Evelyn Harry	February 14	Gather material Write copy Design layout Printing Distribution
Provide workshops for committees	Bill Evelyn *Roosevelt	March 3	Locate place and date Invite participants Acquire training staff Design workshop Conduct it Evaluate
Recruit new team members	Frances *Martin Eilene Harris	April 15	Identify potential members Interview them Invite to an orientation meeting with team Mutual decision on joining

* Key persons.

(3) *Plan to implement the innovation* by: developing time schedules, short and long term; assigning tasks to persons; developing procedures for carrying out plans and monitoring progress; providing for pretesting and pilot evaluation, if appropriate; gathering needed resources; and building links to other persons, issues, or parts of the institution.

(4) *Relate the change to the necessary changes in individuals* by: providing individuals with relevant information; allowing individuals to test their interest and commitment; providing support and training for development of new skills or attitudes; and providing for sharing of accomplishments.

Table 4.

THE SEVEN A'S IN A SUCCESSFUL INDIVIDUAL CHANGE PROCESS

AWARENESS	Does the individual find out about the project?		
↓	Yes	No	Lost
ATTENTION	Is he or she able to obtain enough information?		
↓	Yes	No	Rejected
APPREHENSION	Does he or she overcome doubts and feel good about the project?		
↓	Yes	No	Rejected
ACCEPTANCE	Are the initial tryouts or tests successful?		
↓	Yes	No	Rejected
ADAPTATION	Does he or she have the ability and resources to act?		
↓	Yes	No	Rejected
ACTION	Does the new behavior become integrated into day-to-day behavior?		
↓	Yes	No	Lost
ASSIMILATION			

VI

Connecting to the Organization

The change team and its client are usually part of a larger organization, the college, and they may be able to function relatively independently when all resources needed for change are available within their boundaries; at other times there is great interdependency with the larger organization. In this section we will examine these interdependencies, their effects on the change team, and what the change team needs to do to survive and be effective. In addition to diagnosing the links between the team and its environment, we will provide some ideas about ways of improving these links.

There are three links between the team and the college: communications, resources, and influence. Any of these may be one or two-way connections. In an action-research approach, two-way communication is most desirable. Your team can be outside of the organization, a part of it, or a few key members can link it to the organization.

You will need communication linkages to keep in touch with other persons, parts of the organization, or issues in the external environment. You will need resource linkages to acquire money, time, and space for your group's activities. These resources may be increased by linking together several projects with similar goals. Influence linkages are often critical, however. Many efforts at organizational innovation have been halted by top level decision makers who were not fully appraised of the objectives and procedures of the change team. Management support is especially important if changes in their own attitudes and behavior are required by the change project, or if they suspect the possibility of unwelcome changes.

Your team is a slice of the total campus culture. Many of the stresses, values, and assumptions of this larger culture will be experienced and reflected in the team, such as: political differences, relationships between students, faculty and administration, segregation of departments from one another—all the facts of campus life. Many major events in team history relate directly to the campus culture, and sometimes to the surrounding society. Since the style and performance of your team tends to flow from its environment, it is therefore valuable to understand the environment and the ways it may impinge on the team. Our teams have been profoundly affected by anti-war protests, government decisions on funding, independence movements, and national concern about drug abuse. They have also been influenced by authoritarian and by nondirective administrative styles and by campus climates which were highly structured or in flux.

Relationships within the teams also reflect the tensions on the campus as a whole. Sharp political differences dividing the campus can also divide the team. Where differences in life style exist on the campus, they are likely to be present in the team. Some members of your team also may be disturbed by fears of censure by administration or faculty.

Teams often use their new group setting to compensate for aspects of the environment they do not like. Where the campus environment is bureaucratic and structured, the teams may emphasize interpersonal relations and development of a warm climate. Where the environment is uncertain and ambiguous with respect to the flow of work, the team can provide members with an opportunity to get things done. On a campus with deep political divisions, the ability of the team to function in spite of serious value differences among its members is highly commendable.

How much external connection your team may need will depend on how much support the campus authorities provide. Teams with little support have indicated that association with NTL and with teams from other campuses have been very helpful in providing ideas, motivations, useful criticism, and rewarding social relationships. If your team receives adequate support from significant persons on the campus, you may find that, external connections are less important.

Your team members can become aware of cultural problems and biases by examining their own behavior and questioning to what extent they are really problem-solving as opposed to reflecting a particular attitude. Team members can ask themselves and other team members, "Are you talking as a student, militant, senior professor, administrator, or as a team member?"

Persons to fill at least these three roles are needed in a team. Your members should include: (1) information specialists to obtain and process data about the state of affairs on campus and to develop innovative goals; (2) committed zealots who are prepared to inspire other persons and give the project a charge; and (3) political experts, shakers and movers who know how to get things done in the system. A balance should be developed between these three roles depending, in part, on your team's relationship to its environment. Problems can roll in from two directions. Some teams are too data- and research-oriented, leading to impatience among those who are more committed to action than to knowledge. Or, the results-oriented team may not generate enough data to plan or to test the effects of its actions.

Your team's ability to acquire power may depend on its ability to broaden its perception of power sources. Good connections will help your team to be aware of various influence sources. Initially, teams tend to feel that the only power is that granted by institutional authorities. They can learn there are other power sources, too, such as: collecting and disseminating information that shows the need for change; developing and presenting alternative solutions to problems; organizing students or faculty to support a change; adding to the team persons in power positions; establishing relationships between the team and influential persons; developing liaisons with appropriate committees on campus; and acquiring grants which give the team independent economic resources.

Your team must achieve a balance between its internal cohesiveness and its connections to the campus. If your team becomes isolated and alienated, it will lose its effectiveness. On the other hand, if it is too closely connected to the campus it may lose its drive for originality and creativity. The key concept in analysing this relationship is to examine the similarity of the values of your team and its social environment. Your team needs to be aware of the extent to which it shares the values of the administration, faculty, and student groups. Similarities and discrepancies in values are vital elements in devising change strategies.

When there is some overlap in values, your team can use discrepancies between institutionally-stated values and actual practices as leverage for change. For example, a team which was working on improving student involvement in decision-making was able to gain acquiescence from some reluctant deans and departmental chairmen because the administration's policy supported what it was trying to do.

Where there is insufficient overlapping of values, the conditions for change move toward revolution. For instance, if students believe they are not sufficiently represented in university governance and the administration says no students should be so involved, there is little room for collaborative change efforts. Collaborative strategies include the possibility of using the values and goals of campus groups as levers for change which assumes some common attitudes among them.

The main point is that in a collaborative effort, the strategy for coping with resistance to change is increased collaboration, such as: efforts to gain clarification and understanding, accepting the influence of significant persons and groups, and exploring the causes of differences. Your change team should not be the advocate of a particular solution but should support a process which includes developing a mutually acceptable goal. The path to that goal should be amenable to influence by all parties concerned.

VII

*Using Consultants
and Substitutes*

In this section we will look at relationships between consultants and clients, the roles consultants can play, and what the group can expect from them. These issues are similar to those in the change team and client relationships, which we have already discussed. The skills and knowledge of a good change team are almost the same as the skills and knowledge of a good consultant. For instance, to help a group become more effective, a consultant must assist it to gather and process information about itself, to muster commitment, to devise appropriate actions, and to evaluate results. These are issues for the team in its own work as well as in its dealing with consultants. Therefore, many observations made in this chapter will apply to your team in its work with its own clients.

Client Expectations of Consultant

As was emphasized earlier, your team needs to have a clear understanding of what the consultant is capable of doing and how decisions will be made as to which activities will be provided, when they will be carried out, and what the costs will be. You also can reasonably expect help from your consultant in the following areas:

Climate setting. Assistance is generally needed in setting an atmosphere that will deal adequately with member anxieties and will facilitate the development of a strong, cohesive group.

Helping set priorities. The consultant should be expected to keep set priorities for group action so that things are dealt with in logical sequence and that important issues are not left out or lightly passed over.

Diagnosing needed roles. The consultant should be expected continually to diagnose the need for various roles or functions to be played in your group, and he or she should help get those roles filled.

Building member resources. The consultant should continually attempt to work out of the job by building into group members as many skills as possible.

Reality testing. A consultant can use his perspective to test the feasibility of the ideas and strategies of your group.

Program advocacy. Your group should expect the consultant to be committed to the program and to be an advocate of it both inside and outside the organization.

These expectations should be reviewed from time to time by the consultant and the client group to make sure that the relationship is solidly built and to prevent suspicion, distance, resentments, or disappointments. Since trust is critical to the work of a consultant, you should be aware of anything that would undermine it.

Selection of Consultants

There are a number of issues which need to be looked at openly and agreed upon with the consultant before selecting him or her. The key questions are:

Insider or outsider? Many organizations, especially universities, have people with consulting skills already working for them. Those persons can be used instead of bringing in outside consultants. However, a competent outsider can bring to the group more prestige, motivation, energy-focusing, and risk-taking qualities than can an insider merely because he is not a part of the system. You should ask how important are those factors in conducting your project. (At the end of this section there are some tips on working without outside consultants.)

Cost? The fees of consultants vary considerably depending on their prestige, the client's resources, the consultant's interest in the project, the amount of time involved, and what is expected. Fees range from just enough payment to cover expenses to $1,000 or more per day. Most behavioral scientists who do consulting are paid $150 to $400 per day plus expenses. But an expensive consultant may not necessarily be best for your project, particularly if he or she is a specialist in another field. You should find out what financial resources are available and be candid with a potential consultant about how much you can afford. You should also allow for extra costs if other people in the institution spend time working with consultants.

What connections does the consultant have? A consultant should have access to resources which are relevant to your particular needs such as: other people, materials, training activities, and sources of information. Frequently they can establish mutually useful connections between various projects, as was done in the NTL Campus Change Team project.

Qualifications. An important advantage of bringing in an outside consultant is to add legitimacy and prestige to the change project. Therefore, look at the consultant's background in light of what he can offer to your team. For instance, consultants with high status in an industrial setting do not necessarily have prestige in an academic setting. Further, the nature of many campus change efforts makes it very important that women, minority groups, or young people be engaged in consulting. (A consulting *team* often can achieve desirable mixes.)

Time needed. You should find out if the consultant will be able to devote the amount of time and energy required by your team. In general, relationships which extend over a period of time are more fruitful than one-shot or short-term contacts. Another consideration for both parties is whether the consultant would be expected to respond to immediate requests for service or crisis interventions as opposed to following a fixed schedule.

Level of commitment? Those involved should be clear about

the motivations of the consultant. Ask yourself what he or she wants from a relationship with your team. What does the consultant hope to gain? Is the consultant's level and source of commitment sufficient to meet your needs?

Skills, orientation, and style. Consultants vary in their backgrounds, theories, abilities, interests, and styles. Some consultants are information- and theory-oriented, others are more "here-and-now" or existential. They also vary in terms of whether they are confronting, supportive, or more interested in personal change than in systems change. Does she or he have the requisite supply of "sandpaper" for stimulation and "blankets" for comforting? Some consultants focus on particular issues such as racism or decision-making. Both parties should establish that they share common interests. Another important issue to look at is whether the consultant is oriented to working for change at the individual, the group, or the organizational level.

Trust worthiness. Perhaps the most critical issue is trust. You and others in the group must trust and respect the consultant; if not, his or her usefulness is severely limited. If trust and mutual enjoyment are lacking, an exciting, productive joining of forces is not going to take place.

Contract Setting

Although frequently the role of the consultant emerges gradually and cannot be spelled out in great detail at the initial stage, there are predictable factors in establishing a contract that can be and should be understood from the beginning. The amount of time, the money, and provisions for payment; the degree of responsibility and accountability; and the general nature of the task are some key items to cover. The definition of the role of the consultant should be outlined in general, and provision should be made for modifying or specifying that role in greater detail as the program develops.

Since your consultant probably will have limited time available for your project, it is essential that an understanding be developed as to the resources that will be available from your group, the kind of administration that will be required (and who will carry that out), and the nature of your group's commitment. The consultant may also want to find out the level of group commitment, the tasks the group wishes to work on, and how progress will be evaluated. Failure to set out these terms initially and to update the agreement periodically can hinder your program. Some key factors which need to be considered in building an agreement are outlined below.

Who is the consultant? Although this question may seem obvious at face value, it often turns out to be complicated. If the program is carried out by an individual consultant, there should be clarity about whether any of the consultant's associates, observers, trainees, or colleagues will be involved, and under what conditions or terms such additional persons shall work. In addition, there should be a provision for deciding on a substitute or replacement should the consultant be absent or withdraw from your project. If consultation is to be carried out by a group, it is necessary to specify the composition, structure, and criteria for membership in the group, and what choice you may exercise in choosing who you may use for specific activities.

Who is the client? The client of a consultant may be an individual, a group, an organization, or several subparts of the college. Development of a clear agreement should be made with the contact person, or the leader of an organization, as to the consultant's responsibility to provide individual consultation as opposed to group consultation. Often the interests of the two do not coincide, and the consultant will have to choose where the primary commitment lies—with the group or with the individual.

Who should develop the contract? Whenever possible, the contract should be developed by everyone in both the team and consultant groups who will be directly involved in the program. However, this is often not feasible and in that case the contract will have to be worked out by legitimized representatives. It is then important to agree to test the contract with as many persons as possible before it is finally set.

Confidentiality. A consultant often hears confidential information in the course of his work. There should be a clear identification of what information is to be widely shared and what is to remain confidential. (This issue can be tricky if the consultant is a part of a team. In this case it needs to be clear whether confidential information can be shared among all team members.)

Relation to organization leadership. If your client is a subunit of the college, you should clarify the relationship and responsibility of your client to the college and the degree to which the consultant has access to and can be called upon by college leadership. In general, plan to keep the leadership of your institution informed of your program and the nature of the consulting activities.

Periodic evaluation and review. The relationship between a team and its consultant will change continuously as the program develops. It is essential that provision be made for periodic assessment of that relationship and renegotiation of the original contract.

External guidelines. Frequently external restrictions, policies, and guidelines must be followed by the consultant and your group. These may involve use of facilities, financial procedures, legal requirements, employment provisions, or permissible activities. In so far as possible, these limitations should be noted in advance.

Collaborating organizations. Collaborating organizations or individuals may work with either your teams or the consultant. It is helpful to spell out the roles and relationships between these different parties.

Termination conditions. The conditions under which the contract may be terminated and the rights and responsibilities of each party need to be clearly understood. Generally there is an understanding that either side can terminate the relationship if there is dissatisfaction, but it may be complicated if money or long-term commitments are involved.

Roles and Resources

The primary style of consultation we have used in the action-research program is built around *process orientation,* an approach designed to provide help to a client by facilitating effective teamwork, utilization of resources, development of work skills, and the provision for feedback mechanisms. This style contrasts with consultation that emphasizes the *content* of a change effort. Often it is appropriate to blend process and content together in a consultation, but your prospective consultant should clearly state his primary orientation. Since consulting is definitely an art which entails working with complex mixtures, universal rules do not exist. However, here are some tips to help you proceed when working with process oriented consulting. They will need to be modified as necessary to meet specific circumstances.

Client responsibility for task. The responsibility for direct project work lies with members of your group—not with the consultant, who should consistently reinforce this notion. When a group is floundering, the primary aim of the consultant is to help the group get itself in a position to take corrective action on its own, without stepping in to act directly for the group.

Group membership of consultant. The consultant is a temporary member of your group and should try to minimize your dependency on him or her. One way of promoting team independence is for the consultant to meet with the group occasionally or periodically rather than to attend every meeting.

Consultant as model. The consultant should act as a model for the behaviors which the group is being encouraged to use. These generally include directness, openness, willingness to risk, commitment to follow through on tasks, supportiveness, appropriate confrontation, reliability, high energy level, analytical thinking, and having fun.

Group process focus. Assessment and group maintenance functions need to be developed both for preventing and solving crises. Frequently, the initial skills of action-research teams are better developed in the task area than in the process or group maintenance area. Special training, such as a workshop on group dynamics, can increase group process skills in your group. Consultants can also introduce activities which help the group to learn such skills during regular meetings. For instance, two observers can be selected from the team. They can be given instruction in identifying behaviors which represent a group process orientation and those which represent a task orientation. At twenty-minute intervals, the observers can be given five minutes to report their observations. After three such periods, the group can engage in a discussion of the behaviors and processes which were observed.

Personal growth of members. Wherever possible, the personal learning and development needs of group members should be integrated into their task work. This integration requires spending time to understand and respond to individual needs. The consultant can help to legitimize such activities. For instance, one way of responding to individual needs is to assign members tasks that develop competence rather than to assign tasks to those who can already perform them well.

Participation and involvement. Changes can be generated by active participation of the people in the system being changed. Members of an action-research team need to develop skills to encourage the participation and involvement of people who are in the organization which they are trying to change so that they will develop ownership of the goals and strategies. The consultant can help the team to develop those attitudes and skills.

Helping set direction. During the goal-setting process, the consultant frequently can help your group to avoid the twin traps of moving into action prematurely or of studying the issues to the point where energy for moving is lost.

Developing a functional organization. It is often helpful to provide variety in ways to carry out tasks. For example, many groups are not used to using temporary subgroups, or rotating leadership, or to defining group roles based on needed functions, or to avoiding building hierarchies, or to using an explicit problem-solving process. These are all alternatives which your group can consider if it is aware of them.

Providing information. It is important for your consultant to suggest other approaches, strategies, or sources of technical material so that your group does not labor unnecessarily without knowledge of work already carried out by other groups or individuals.

Building enthusiasm and support. It is essential that your project becomes enjoyable as well as worthwhile. Volunteer groups normally will not stick to drudgery very long. The consultant can often provide encouragement—and a sense of humor can help a group to deal with the inevitable low points or negative aspects of its work.

Providing legitimacy. A consultant can bring prestige to a project either through his individual reputation or through his affiliation with an outside organization. People usually attribute more status to outsiders than to their own members, even if the insider's skill is as great as the outsider's.

Building discipline. The periodic visits of a consultant—who may ask "What's happening?"—provide incentive for members to complete task work and take their responsibilities seriously. Thus consultant visits may help members to utilize their time better because of their interest in making the best use of him or her.

Helping with crises or high-risk activities. By being less identified with an organization and being less caught up in the culture, an outside consultant is in a good position to help solve a crisis. Similarly, the consultant can encourage your group to avoid becoming overly cautious and conservative and can take over critical roles when there is a need for a potentially expendable person— and this is a risk that an internal group member cannot take. (One of the main assets of a consultant should be expendability!)

The balance and emphasis of these different activities will obviously depend on the particular needs of your group and the talents of the consultant. Also, a good way to reduce dependency on the consultant is for the group to have an active part in determining what the consultant will do and in evaluating his or her impact.

Working Without Consultants

As we have said, outside consultants have advantages over persons who are members of the college organization. Teams, however, do not always have the money to hire a consultant and other reasons, too, may make bringing in outsiders impractical. Furthermore, groups or individuals often will seek assistance from other on-campus persons. Therefore, some thoughts about working without outside consultation are in order.

Using group members. Teams without access to outside consultants can do several things to achieve their objectives. Members of your group can be given the responsibility for making process observations and periodically sharing these with the group. (It helps to have have two people at a time in this role.) Similarly, team members can assume responsibility for leading the group in developmental activities such as those mentioned in Section IX. These roles can be rotated among members. It is crucial, however, that the team be explicit about giving legitimacy to persons who will be filling these roles. It helps if specific meetings or parts of meetings are set aside for team development.

Dangers in using group members as process-orientation persons are that other members may develop resentment over their criticism; such persons' other participation is limited, which they or the group may not like; process persons may feel very vulnerable and not enjoy the experience. These risks can be mitigated by group discussion. If well designed, the experience can be exciting and full of learning.

Using other on-campus resources. On-campus people who are not team members can be asked to help your group on either a specific or an on-going basis. Insiders who are not group members can perform many functions of off-campus consultants (assuming, of course, that they have appropriate skills). One of the strengths of the University of Massachusetts Applied Behavioral Science Alliance has been its ability to supply on-campus consultants to a number of projects on campus. Frequently, these persons work in combination with an off-campus consultant. This combination is ideal; but even without an outside consultant, Alliance members have provided skillful and valuable consulting resources.

Part of the objective of most change teams has been the improvement of their own consulting skills. With this capability, the team is able to assist other groups or individuals. For instance, a team working on student involvement in decision-making has provided consulting for departmental advisory committees. They have designed and run workshops, collected and fed back data, conducted interviews, consulted with individual committee members, produced and distributed written materials, and participated in meetings. These services have made a significant difference in the functioning of the departmental committees.

Going to workshops. Teams can go to workshops which provide information and skills. A number of organizations sponsor events for those who wish to work on organization development, team building, consultation skills, and personal growth. Note, however, that if only a part of your team attends such an event, there is a real risk of creating divisions between those who go and those who stay at home. By all means have the entire group participate in planning what those who go to the event will do and how they will be reintegrated after their return.

VIII

Action-Oriented Research

In this section we deal with the contribution of research to the team, the goals of research, and the expectations of research users. Although this section parallels our discussion of using consultants, Section VII, it is devoted to one particular aspect of the consultant role: helping the team to develop an explicit record of the process it is moving through. This record is developed through a process of collecting, storing, organizing, and interpreting data which may range from describing conditions in the campus environment to articulating the feelings of team members. It may also vary from data gathered by highly rigorous methods to the sharing and recording of impressions of team members.

In our thinking, research is more than a set of formal procedures for advancing a body of knowledge. It is a process whereby a social unit guides its actions. For your team to be effective, it must increase its capacity to formulate maps which direct its actions and organize its experiences.

Contribution to Team

Teams usually do not have a clear sense of the need for available knowledge or collecting data. The needs to gain commitment and develop action plans are felt more keenly and are more satisfying. In fact, team members often have a negative veiw of research; they regard the time and energy required to collect and to organize data as barriers to effective commitment and action. Let us examine in detail this relation of research to commitment and to action.

Knowledge and commitment. Most people see knowledge as confirming or disconfirming their beliefs about how they or others should behave without seeing neutral facts. Your team member who learns that others on his team tend to regard him as overly critical of them should be interested in both the reality of this fact and in its social significance. Similarly, the group that sees itself fighting—or flighting—whenever the task becomes difficult also should evaluate that behavior. Facts about the way the campus operates can be viewed from two perspectives: as information and in terms of standards of how the campus should be operating. If research reveals that there are no women full professors in a university, there are both descriptive and emotional components to this information —which can generate action. Knowledge has both factual and evaluative implications: it points out reality and it also can influence one's commitment to change aspects of that reality.

Knowledge and action. An effective team will increase its ability to collect and synthesize knowledge, to link this knowledge to the development of goals, and move into action. The role of knowledge is steering or control; it indicates both the facts and the deviance of these facts from expectations. This deviance, if seen as serious, leads to the development of ideas for remedying the situation and then to corrective action. For example, if your students believe they should have some option to select courses in their freshman year and find they have none, they are challenged to examine the validity of their beliefs or their capacity to enforce changes to fit their beliefs. (Clearly, however, the greater the power of the person or social unit, the greater the ability to change the environment to square with one's beliefs rather than to adjust one's beliefs to the setting.)

Knowledge and power. Knowledge becomes power only when it is effectively linked to action. Conversely, the capacity of a team to steer its actions depends partly on its ability to acquire and use knowledge. Data collected by your team can help them with their tasks and also help them to organize themselves effectively and enjoyably. A continual cycle of research, evaluation, and action can provide a change model for the substantive issues on which your group is working. It also can provide a model for team tasks (such as recruiting, selecting, and integrating new members; developing useful and enjoyable relationships; and building the relationship between the team and its clients).

Goals and Expectations

The goals of the action-researcher are to increase the control of action through knowledge. We discuss here various methods for achieving these goals.

Linking available social science knowledge and methods to the project. The research specialist can provide findings from prior studies that serve as guides to action. He or she also can be expected to help you select and develop techniques for collecting and interpreting data obtained through surveys and interviews. Our teams have used a variety of research methods to gather information about grading practices, teaching, racism, sexism, organizational behavior, group dynamics, counseling, drugs, and curriculum development.

Increasing team members' knowledge and research skills. The research specialist should be attempting to increase the ability of your team to conceptualize the issues it is confronting and to use action-research methods. Research specialists should exemplify the behaviors which they want team members to use, as pointed out in Section VII. They should build a collaborative relationship with project members in data collection and data processing. They should also explain how to use data to guide and evaluate major project activities (such as a long, intensive meeting; a specific action; or a workshop). Another of the tasks is to develop ways to help your group make sense of its experiences. Finally, research specialists should emphasize the need for data and relevant theory to make diagnoses and to evaluate outcomes.

Skill training sessions can be used in specific research areas (such as knowledge retrieval, collecting data, and using data in planning for change and in evaluating the effects of change). We have provided training in interviewing, questionnaire construction, data analysis, organization of information, and designing evaluation procedures.

Linking project to knowledge in external environment. The research specialist, in collaboration with your team, should continually monitor the entire change process, which includes the growth and development of your team, the specific outcomes of its innovative project, and the impact of the project on the campus environment. The impact of your project can be increased by communicating its results, both substantive and procedural, to various audiences: other project teams which need guidelines for their own actions; education specialists who are interested in new modes of knowing and doing and who want to compare project teams to other methods of institutional reform; project sponsors in agencies which fund activities; institutional sponsors who are concerned with evaluating the impact of project teams on their own institutions and on their own interests; consultants who want to know what strategies and techniques were effective in working with project teams; action-researchers who are interested in the development of action-oriented research techniques; and social scientists who are interested in planned change.

It is valuable to acquire knowledge from other sources which will help you solve problems and avoid pitfalls. Such sources are consultants, on-campus persons with relevant skill or knowledge, a review of the literature, visits to or from other campuses, and workshops.

Assessment Methods

As your team moves along, you will need to answer questions such as: Where is our team located now? Where should we move next? and How do we get there?

To answer these questions, we have designed and adapted a number of ways of documenting team progress and effectiveness. The assessment technology varies in terms of (1) what information is collected and by whom; (2) how data are interpreted and by whom; and (3) how information is fed back and by whom. Three kinds of assessment will be discussed: consultant-directed, shared, and team-directed.

Consultants in data collection feedback role. First, your consultant can provide strategic reviews that cover all aspects of team-task relationships without going into great detail on any one point. In this procedure, your team can collect data by interview, questionnaire, or observation; it is summarized by the consultant and reported back to your team at a meeting called for that purpose. These summaries may be presented on mimeographed sheets or large easel-size paper. However, the longer the delay between data collection and feedback, the less relevant your team will find the information—by all means you should make this period as short as possible.

Some data summaries that we have found helpful are: strengths and weaknesses of the team, comparison between the team and other teams, and comparison between the team at present and at a previous date.

In the feedback procedure, you may find it helpful to warm up team members by asking them to say, one at a time, how they feel about the way things are going. This provides the consultant with a bridge between the summarized data and the members' feelings. He or she can then point out similarities, differences, or additions from the research. Following the feedback, your team should spend some time digesting the material, asking questions, or raising problems. Then you will be ready to discuss the implications of the data.

In addition to periodic strategic reviews, a consultant can design assessment procedures for major activities, such as a long workshop. Your participants should be given a prior opportunity to contribute to program planning. You may query the team by telephone or by brief, mailed questionnaires. At the beginning of the workshop, it is also important for your participants to express their expectations and hopes for the workshop and to compare them to those of other members of their team and to other teams. These shared expectations help to build a unity of purpose which frequently is not recognized at the beginning of a workshop. This procedure sets a standard of active responsibility on the part of all participants for determining the goals of the conference and working to achieve them. There are three ways the assessment can be conducted. (1) A brief questionnaire filled out by each participant can be rapidly summarized by an "assessment team" and fed back

to the entire group at a general session early in the workshop. (2)
Each team can discuss its expectations and then one participant
from each group can report to the workshop. (3) Across-team
groups can discuss their goals, list them on large sheets of newsprint, and post them for all to read.

Periodic analysis of effectiveness and satisfaction with the
conference can help with replanning the remaining time. This can
be accomplished by asking members of the group to check a brief
post-meeting reaction sheet at the end of each session; or, one member of each team can be given the responsibility for observing the
workshop process. The observer group then periodically holds group
evaluation sessions in which they report their observations and suggestions are made for improvements. Another method of periodic
review is to have participants break up into small post-session groups
to evaluate the previous session. Again, a recorder can be appointed
to note his group's reactions and to report them at a general session.

A final evaluation at the end of a workshop should be made.
The procedures can vary from data collection by the staff and feedback after the workshop to the entire group so that participants may
hear and react to the assessments. A variant of the buzz-group
technique can be useful. This involves identifying the major objectives of the workshop and breaking the workshop into six-person
groups that meet to discuss and assess one specific objective of the
workshop each. Again, recorders are appointed for each group and
the findings are summarized in a general session.

Shared consultant-team assessment. In workshops to diagnose
the team, assessment procedures also are conducted jointly by consultants and team members. We have successfully used the following
procedures:

(1) Force field analysis. At a team meeting, members are
asked to identify factors both helping and hindering your team
efforts; these are listed on easel-size newsprint. The presence of a
consultant often enables group members to bring up items that were
too touchy to express without his support. Your team then can point
out one or more hindering forces to try to reduce. The next step is
group problem-solving to devise strategies for achieving that end.

(2) Problem census. Another technique is to list the problems your team faces, assign them priorities, and devise action steps

to remedy them. It is crucial to move to action planning or team members can become very discouraged. Group-strength census can help to build perspective into this process.

(3) Group diagnostic matrix. We have devised a tool which can be helpful in assessment and planning. This instrument (Table 5) is described in Section IX.

Team-directed assessment. The sharing of assessment procedures by consultants and team members will vary with the amount of consultant time available and the assessment skills of team members. Generally, your team must be responsible for tactical reviews of its own process. Some simple procedures are described below.

(1) Allotment of review time at end of meeting. Your team should allot some time at the end of each meeting for each member to discuss and answer the questions: How do you feel about this meeting and about the way things are going generally? How do you feel about the role you are playing in the team? How do you react to others' behavior?

(2) Post-meeting questionnaires. You can provide your team with short post-meeting questionnaires to be filled out anonymously. A subgroup can summarize and feed back the results. This procedure enables participants to communicate feelings and reactions they find difficult to express in the group sessions; the summaries will indicate the extent to which their reactions are shared. The results should then be discussed.

(3) Review of critical incidents. A simple technique for reviewing progress is to look at the critical events in your group's experience; events that members felt strongly about or were turning points. Recall of these highlights provides an opportunity for the group to review where they have been and to make plans for the future.

Assigning resources to assessment. A critical question is how much time and energy you should allocate to assessment activities. These are some likely periods for assesment:

(1) When initiating a new activity, such as inducting new members or beginning a new task.

(2) At the beginning of the school year, or after other vacations. (Your team can particularly profit from an assessment period then.)

(3) When completing an activity, such as a membership drive, a workshop, or a survey.

(4) At crisis times when team activities are halted or seem inadequate. (These crises may be caused by outside events, such as strikes, or by inside events, such as conflict over strategy.)

IX

Designs for Facilitating Team Development

Rather than compiling a catalogue of exercises, we now are going to describe a style of working with a team. This "flow" is presented in the first part of this section along with some specific activities. Further activities related to specific issues can be found in sections II, III, IV, V, VI, VII, and VIII. Some sources for group development instruments and activities will be presented at the end of this section.

The phases which we normally go through in working with a team are shifted, modified, or omitted as circumstances indicate. As with any training endeavor, the activities should respond to the particular needs of the group at a point in time. But it is useful to have in mind an overall pattern within which one can work.

Typical Flow

Developing clear goals. Building an agenda for the meeting is a common first step for a task group. It is helpful to have large sheets of paper with marking pencils (or a blackboard and chalk) to record the ideas for agenda items. The group can then select and schedule the items to be dealt with in its meeting. The items left over should have some future action plan attached to them. Both task and group maintenance issues should be listed. It often helps to use the diagnostic matrix (Table 5). From a more general perspective, the design for a particular session can be agreed upon.

Identifying issues. One consistent intervention which we make with teams is to help them to identify what the issues are at a particular point. Sometimes the concerns are so apparent to everyone that it is unnecessary to focus on them. On the other hand, you will find it frequently useful to go through a procedure which will help members to look at and share where they and the group are. Table 5 can help you move toward those ends. We also have had teams do analyses of the forces which are moving them toward their goal and those which are blocking them (force-field analysis). Members of your group can nonverbally express their current relationships to each other and explore the meanings of their creations. (We have asked members to draw pictures showing how they perceive their relationship to the team and the college. These pictures are then explained and discussed.)

Dealing with feelings of members. Since we often encourage members to express and to explore their feelings about what is happening to them and to the team, it is particularly important to deal with those feelings which may block the work of the group. (But it is not always necessary to deal with all of the interpersonal relationships.) Consultants or process observers can help in identifying and dealing with such feelings.

Here is a useful way to surface and to deal with issues between members. Have each member identify others with whom he or she has an issue to work out. Members then can get together in a pair or small clusters to work on these issues. During these discussions, individuals can build contracts with each other to govern their relationships. Your total group should then come together and listen to reports of what happened.

Organizing for work. It is good to examine how your group can be best organized. You can make a list on a large sheet of paper of various needed functions (such as: building agendas, calling meetings, chairing meetings, maintaining group history, communicating with members, contacting other groups or individuals, process observation, data collection, writing proposals, and carrying out planned actions). These functions can then be built into member roles based on their interests and abilities. Often it is also helpful to set up subgroups which can work simultaneously on different aspects of the task (making sure that there are good mechanisms for keeping the groups linked together as needed). You will find that occasional long meetings (an afternoon and evening, or all day Saturday) are very helpful. (Teams which only meet for an hour or so every other week have a hard time covering both task and group process issues.)

Specific planning. Development of flow charts, time lines, planning matrices, resource allocation plans, task assignments, follow-up programs, and evaluation methods are crucial aspects of a task group's success. We frequently urge groups to engage in such processes and suggest how to do them. You may find it helpful to make plans for specific activities, set deadlines for completion of projects, have members assign themselves to tasks (and pick out the key person). Put everything in writing. Follow-up, coordination, and evaluation processes should then be built into the plan. (See Table 3, Section V.)

Developing perspective. Contact with other teams is very useful in developing perspective on where your team is. Programs which other teams attend, or workshops with two or more teams, provide opportunities for teams to observe each other in action and thus give them new points of view and new skills. We have also used teams as consultants to each other—a rich learning experience for all parties. Other ways of gaining perspective are: consultant feedback, reading about other groups, sending representatives to other groups, inviting visitors from other teams, or attending conferences.

A particularly trying problem is dealing with teams when they are at a low ebb emotionally. All teams go through periods of discouragement and frustration. Maintaining perspective at these points is particularly important. To help to get out of the doldrums, you may contact other teams, for it shows your experience is not unique and is manageable. A presentation by a consultant or a team member about the difficulties of change can also help. Brainstorming a list of your team's task and process achievements can uplift its spirits. Clarification of short-range goals can increase your group's sense of the possible. In any case, an open discussion is an essential starting point.

Providing personal growth experiences. Many teams desire and benefit from activities which promote individual's learning about themselves and their relations with others. We have used a variety of verbal and nonverbal activities toward that end. For instance, fantasies, body movement, role playing, drawing, small self-awareness groups, meditation, and life planning exercises can be worked to advantage into a team's experience. Our assumption is that increasing the personal and interpersonal competence of members will increase the potency of your team.

Reflecting and evaluating. As stressed previously, your team needs to have an orderly process to gather and to consider data about its own performance. It is important to have that process firmly built into the life of the group because there is a strong tendency in the press of task work to skip such reflection. Inside persons can have monitoring and feedback as a part of their roles. The group can agree to a regular procedure, such as spending twenty minutes at the end of each meeting looking at its own process. Consultants, of course, usually have this function as one of their main activities. (We have used questionnaires, interviews, and observations as methods of gathering information to feed back to the group. The feedback is more useful when it is built into a group discussion which moves from diagnosis to remedial action.)

Diagnosing Needs

Two sets of concepts describe the functioning of change teams. One set relates to the phases of change and the other to the tasks which need to be performed. These categories are organized in Table 5, which is useful in looking at the history and progress of your team. It can also be used as a diagnostic tool for planning by identifying areas of strength and weakness in the team, setting priorities for the team's attention, and helping team members and consultants to get an orderly view of the state of the team. Descriptions of the headings in Table 5 follow.

Develop the goal. Perhaps the most powerful aspect of planning for change is getting a clear idea or image of how you would like the future to differ from the present. It is important to set a clear and realistic goal about which there is agreement in the group, and which is felt to be worthwhile.

Develop resources. Attention, time, energy, money, and power must be generated in order to realize the goal.

Move to action. Taking action involves diagnosis of problems, selecting likely points of entry, designing actions, and taking steps to implement them.

Building membership. Recruiting and developing members who have the needed interests, skills, commitment, and connections.

Team development. Developing a team that has good decision-making processes, one that can solve problems, coordinate its activities, and provide satisfaction for its members.

Organization linkages. For example, links to the faculty, a department, student government, deans, or interest groups.

Working on projects. For example, holding workshops, gathering data, conducting data feedback sessions, establishing a counseling program, organizing action groups, initiating organization development activities, creating a new academic program, and designing a new governance process.

Self-renewal. Providing long-range planning and evaluations, and proceeding with tasks in ways which help the growth of the individuals and groups involved.

We have found in use of this diagnostic and planning tool as a group exercise, that it is frequently better at first to use only the columns (basic tasks) and ignore, for the moment, Change phases. To use all of the boxes initially is too complex. We suggest that you divide your group into trios; have each trio list the positive and negative aspects of the team under each of the categories: Building Membership, Team Development, Organization Linkages, Working on Projects, and Self-renewal. Then have each trio report its conclusions with a recorder summarizing the points on a board or a large sheet of paper which has the task headings across the top. Under each heading, list the positive points at the top of the column and the negative points at the bottom. This overview will highlight the strengths and weaknesses of the team. A particular problem

Table 5.

GROUP DIAGNOSIS MATRIX

Change Phases	Basic Tasks				
	Building Membership	*Team Development*	*Organization Linkages*	*Working on Projects*	*Self-renewal*
Develop the goals					
Develop resources					
Move to action					

area, such as lack of links to other parts of the organization, can then be selected for attention. Your group can move on to develop goals, resources, and action plans for dealing with that problem.

Selected Sources for Exercises and Activities

The asterisked publications in the Bibliography are rich resources for ideas and techniques about things to do to help a group in its own development. Consultants can be expected to have their own inventories of appropriate and useful things to do. A final point: A team working on its own can use one or more of its members to lead the group in team-building or personal growth activities. But you should be sure to provide specific legitimization for persons to provide such leadership. Also, build in a review of how the session went and feed back to the leader.

Bibliography

Asterisked items are especially rich resources for tactical ideas and techniques for team development.

ADAMS, J. D. (Ed.) *Theory and Method in Organization Development: An Evolutionary Process.* Arlington, Va.: NTL Institute for Applied Behavioral Science, 1974.

ARGYRIS, C. *Personality and Organization.* New York: Harper and Row, 1957.

ARGYRIS, C. *Integrating the Individual and the Organization.* New York: Wiley, 1964.

AXELROD, J. "The Creative Student and the Grading System." In P. Heist (Ed.), *The Creative College Student: An Unmet Challenge.* San Francisco: Jossey-Bass, 1968.

BECKHARD, R. *Organization Development: Strategies and Models.* Reading, Mass.: Addison-Wesley, 1969.

BENEDICT, B. A., CALDER, P. H., CALLAHAN, D. M., HORNSTEIN, H. A. AND MILES, M. B. "The Clinical Experimental Approach to Assessing Organizational Change Efforts." *Journal of Applied Behavioral Science,* 1967, *3*(3), 347–349.

BENNIS, W., *Changing Organizations.* New York: McGraw-Hill, 1966.

BION, W. R. *Experiences in Groups.* New York: Basic Books, 1961.

BLAKE, R. R., AND MOUTON, J. S. *Building a Dynamic Corporation Through Grid Organization Development.* Reading, Mass.: Addison-Wesley, 1969.

173

BLUMBERG, A. *Sensitive Training: Processes, Problems and Applications.* Syracuse, N.Y.: Syracuse University Publications in Continuing Education, 1971.

BRADFORD, L. P., GIBB, J. R., AND BENNE, K. D. (Eds.) *T-Group Theory and Laboratory Method: Innovation in Re-Education.* New York: Wiley, 1964.

BRUYN, S. T. *The Human Perspective in Sociology.* Englewood Cliffs, N.J.: Prentice-Hall, 1966.

BUNKER, D. R., AND KNOWLES, E. S. "Comparison of Behavioral Changes Resulting from Human Relations Training Laboratories of Different Lengths." *Journal of Applied Behavioral Science,* 1967, *3*(4), 505–524.

BURKE, W. W., AND HORNSTEIN, H. A. (Eds.) *The Social Technology of Organization Development.* Fairfax, Va.: NTL Learning Resources Corp., 1972.

BURTON, A. (Ed.) *Encounter.* San Francisco: Jossey-Bass, 1969.

CAMPBELL, J. P., AND DUNNETE, M. D. "Effectiveness of T-Group Experiences in Managerial Training and Development." *Psychological Bulletin,* 1968, *70,* 73–104.

Carnegie Commission. *The Purposes and the Performance of Higher Education in the United States.* New York: McGraw-Hill, 1973.

CHICKERING, A. *Education and Identity.* San Francisco: Jossey-Bass, 1971.

CLARK, B. R. *The Distinctive College: Antioch, Reed and Swarthmore.* Chicago: Aldine, 1970.

CREAGER, J. A. *Selective Policies and Practices in Higher Education.* Washington, D.C.: American Council on Education, 1973.

CROSS, K. P. *Beyond the Open Door.* San Francisco: Jossey-Bass, 1971.

DANIELS, A. K., KAHN-HUT, R., AND ASSOCIATES. *Academics on the Line.* San Francisco: Jossey-Bass, 1970.

DRUCKER, P. F. "On Managing the Public Service Institution." *The Public Interest,* fall 1973, *33,* 43–60.

DYER, W. G. (Ed.) *Modern Theory and Method in Group Training.* New York: Van Nostrand Reinhold, 1972.

Employment of High School Graduates and Dropouts. Washington, D.C.: Bureau of Labor Statistics, Oct. 1972.

ETZIONI, A. "Authority Structure and Organizational Effectiveness." *Administrative Science Quarterly,* 1959, *4*(1).

ETZIONI, A. *The Active Society.* New York: Free Press, 1968.

EVANS, R. I. *Resistance to Innovation in Higher Education.* San Francisco: Jossey-Bass, 1970.

FAIRWEATHER, G. W. *Methods for Experimental Social Innovation.* New York: Wiley, 1967.

FELDMAN, K. A., AND NEWCOMB, T. M. *The Impact of College on Students.* San Francisco: Jossey-Bass, 1969.

FLOURNOY, D. M., AND ASSOCIATES. *The New Teachers.* San Francisco: Jossey-Bass, 1972.

FREEDMAN, M. B. *The College Experience.* San Francisco: Jossey-Bass, 1967.

FRIEDLANDER, F. "A Comparative Study of Consulting Processes and Group Development." *Journal of Applied Behavioral Science,* 1968, *4*(4), 377–401.

FRIEDLANDER, F. "The Primacy of Trust as a Facilitator of Further Group Accomplishment." *Journal of Applied Behavioral Science,* 1970, *6*(4), 387–400.

GARDNER, J. W. *Self-Renewal: The Individual and the Innovative Society.* New York: Harper and Row, 1963.

GLEASON, R. "A Dialogue on Creativity." In P. Heist (Ed.), *The Creative College Student: An Unmet Challenge.* San Francisco: Jossey-Bass, 1968.

GLIDEWELL, J. C. *Choice Points.* Cambridge, Mass.: MIT Press, 1970.

GOLEMBIEWSKI, R. T., AND BLUMBERG, A. (Eds.) *Sensitivity Training and the Laboratory Approach.* Itasca, Ill.: Peacock, 1970.

HALL, J. "The Use of Instruments in Laboratory Training." *Training and Development Journal,* 1970, *24*(5), 48–55.

HALL, L., AND ASSOCIATES. *New Colleges for New Students.* San Francisco: Jossey-Bass, 1974.

HAMPDEN-TURNER, C. M. "An Existential 'Learning Theory' and the Integration of T-Group Research." *Journal of Applied Behavioral Science,* 1966, *2*(4), 367–386.

HARE, A. P. *Handbook of Small Group Research.* New York: Free Press, 1962.

HARRISON, R. "Classroom Innovation: A Design Primer." In P. Runkel, R. Harrison, and M. Runkel (Eds.), *The Changing College Classroom.* San Francisco: Jossey-Bass, 1969.

HAVELOCK, R. G. *Planning for Innovation Through Dissemination and Utilization of Knowledge.* Ann Arbor, Mich.: Institute for Social Research, University of Michigan, 1970.

HAVELOCK, R. G., AND BENNE, K. D. "An Exploratory Study of Knowledge Utilization." In G. Watson (Ed.), *Concepts for Social Change*. Washington, D.C.: NTL, NEA, 1967.

HEFFERLIN, J. L. *The Dynamics of Academic Reform*. San Francisco: Jossey-Bass, 1969.

HEIST, P. (Ed.) *The Creative College Student: An Unmet Challenge*. San Francisco: Jossey-Bass, 1968.

HENDERSON, A. D. *The Innovative Spirit*. San Francisco: Jossey-Bass, 1970.

HODGKINSON, H. L., AND MEETH, L. R. (Eds.) *Power and Authority*. San Francisco: Jossey-Bass, 1971.

HODGKINSON, H. L., AND BLOY, M. B., JR. (Eds.) *Identity Crisis in Higher Education*. San Francisco: Jossey-Bass, 1971.

HOFFER, E. *The Ordeal of Change*. New York: Harper and Row, 1963.

HORNSTEIN, H. A., BUNKER, B. B., BURKE, W. W., GINDES, M., AND LEWICKI, R. J. (Eds.) *Social Intervention: A Behavioral Science Approach*. New York: Free Press, 1971.

HOUSE, R. J. "T-Group Education and Leadership Effectiveness: A Review of the Empirical Literature and a Critical Evaluation." *Personnel Psychology*, 1967, *20*, 1–32.

HOWARD, J. *Please Touch*. New York: McGraw-Hill, 1970.

JAQUES, E. "Social Therapy: Technocracy or Collaboration." *Journal of Social Issues*, 1947, *3*(2).

JEROME, J. *Culture Out of Anarchy*. New York: Herder and Herder, 1970.

* JOHNSON, D. W. *Reaching Out*. Englewood Cliffs, N.J.: Prentice-Hall, 1973. Primarily for an audience of young people but contains a wealth of activities together with research results and theories about interpersonal relations.

JONES, R. *Fantasy and Feeling in Education*. New York: New York University Press, 1968.

KATZ, D., AND KAHN, R. L. *The Social Psychology of Organizations*. New York: Wiley, 1966.

KEETON, M. *Shared Authority on Campus*. Washington, D.C.: American Association for Higher Education, 1971.

KEETON, M., AND HILBERRY, C. *Struggle and Promise: A Future for Colleges*. New York: McGraw-Hill, 1969.

KEETON, M. T. *Models and Mavericks*. New York: McGraw-Hill, 1971.

KENISTON, K. *Young Radicals*. New York: Harcourt Brace Jovanovich, 1968.

KLEIN, D. "Some Notes on the Dynamics of Resistance to Change: The

Defender Role." In G. Watson (Ed.), *Concepts for Social Change*. Washington, D.C.: NTL, NEA, 1967.

KROEBER, T. "Confronting Irreconcilable Issues." In A. K. Daniels, R. Kahn-Hut, Associates, *Academics on the Line*. San Francisco: Jossey-Bass, 1970.

* LAKE, D. G., MILES, M. B., AND EARLE, R. B., JR. (Eds.) *Measuring Human Behavior*. New York: Teachers College Press, 1973. Information about eighty-four instruments for individual and group measurements.

LAKIN, M. "Some Ethical Issues in Sensitivity Training." *American Psychologist*, 1969, *24*, 923–928.

LAWRENCE, P. R., AND LORSCH, J. W. *Developing Organizations: Diagnosis and Action*. Reading, Mass.: Addison-Wesley, 1969.

LEWIN, K. "Frontiers in Group Dynamics." *Human Relations*, 1947, *1*(1), 5–42.

LEWIN, K. *Resolving Social Conflict*. New York: Harper and Row, 1948.

LEWIN, K. *Field Theory in Social Sciences*. New York: Harper and Row, 1951.

LEWIN, K., AND OTHERS. "Levels of Aspiration." In J. M. V. Hunt (Ed.), *Personality and Behavior Disorders*. New York: Ronald Press, 1944.

LIEBERMAN, M. A., YALOM, I. D., AND MILES, M. B. *Encounter Groups: First Facts*. New York: Basic Books, 1973.

LIKERT, R. *The Human Organization: Its Management and Value*. New York: McGraw-Hill, 1967.

LIPPITT, R. "The Use of Social Research to Improve Social Practice." In G. Watson (Ed.), *Concepts for Social Change*. Washington, D.C.: NTL, NEA, 1967.

LIPPITT, R., WATSON, J., AND WESTLEY, B. *The Dynamics of Planned Change*. New York: Harcourt Brace Jovanovich, 1958.

* LUFT, J. *Of Human Interaction*. Palo Alto, Calif.: National Press Books, 1969. Extensive discussion of the theory of self-disclosure and feedback as a learning process, using the JOHARI window as a model. Examples of applications for individuals and for groups.

MARROW, A. J., BOWERS, D. G., AND SEASHORE, S. E. *Management by Participation*. New York: Harper and Row, 1967.

MARTIN, W. B. "How Administrators View Innovation." *Change*, Sept. 1973, p. 51.

MAYHEW, L. B. *The Carnegie Commission on Higher Education.* San Francisco: Jossey-Bass, 1973.

MEETH, R. "Administrators and Leadership." In H. L. Hodgkinson and R. Meeth (Eds.), *Power and Authority.* San Francisco: Jossey-Bass, 1971.

* MILES, M. B. *Learning to Work in Groups.* New York: Bureau of Publications, Teachers College, Columbia University, 1959. Presentation of theories and experiences with groups. Many ideas about things to do to diagnose and to deal with problems.

MILES, M. B. (Ed.) *Innovation in Education.* New York: Bureau of Publications, Teachers College, Columbia University, 1964.

* MILL, C. R. (Ed.) *Twenty Exercises for Trainers.* Fairfax, Va.: NTL Learning Resources Corp., n.d. Each exercise includes a description of its purpose, appropriate setting, procedures, and ways of analyzing results. Group, intergroup, and individual activities are included.

* MILL, C. R., AND PORTER, L. C. (Eds.) *Reading Book for Laboratories in Human Relations Training.* Arlington, Va.: NTL Institute, 1972. A collection of papers about concepts and processes relating to group behavior, personal learning, planned change, and consultation.

MILLER, R. I. *Evaluating Faculty Performance.* San Francisco: Jossey-Bass, 1972.

MILTON, O. *Alternatives to the Traditional.* San Francisco: Jossey-Bass, 1973.

NAPIER, R. W., AND GERSHENFELD, M. K. *Groups: Theory and Experience.* Boston: Houghton Mifflin, 1973.

* NYLEN, D., MITCHELL, J. R., AND STOUT, A. *Handbook of Staff Development and Human Relations Training.* Arlington, Va.: NTL Institute for Applied Behavioral Science, 1967. Collection of lecture materials, exercises, and discussion of the work of group trainers. Considerable emphasis on intergroup and intercultural issues.

* PFEIFFER, J. W., AND JONES, J. E. *A Handbook of Structured Experiences.* Vols. 1–4. Iowa City, Iowa: University Associates Press, 1969, 1970, 1971, 1972. Collections of exercises of all kinds. Very little discussion of how or when to use them or what theories underlie them, but a wealth of suggestions about things to do.

* PFEIFFER, J. W., AND JONES, J. E. (Eds.) *The Annual Handbook for*

Group Facilitators. Iowa City, Iowa: University Associates Press, 1972, 1973. Exercises, lecture materials, instruments, theories, annotated bibliography, and descriptions of training resources are included.

RASKIN, M. *Being and Doing.* New York: Random House, 1971.

RICE, A. K. "Individual, Group, and Interpersonal Processes." *Human Relations,* 1969, *22*(6), 565–584.

ROGERS, C. *Freedom to Learn.* Columbus, Ohio: Merrill, 1969.

ROGERS, C. *Carl Rogers on Encounter Groups.* New York: Harper and Row, 1970.

ROURKE, F. E., AND BROOKS, G. E. *The Managerial Revolution in Higher Education.* Baltimore: Johns Hopkins Press, 1966.

RUNKLE, R., HARRISON, R., AND RUNKLE, M. (Eds.) *The Changing College Classroom.* San Francisco: Jossey-Bass, 1969.

SARASON, S. B. *The Creation of Settings and the Future Societies.* San Francisco: Jossey-Bass, 1972.

SASHKIN, M., MORRIS, W. C., AND HORST, L. "A Comparison of Social and Organizational Change Models: Information Flow and Data Use Processes." *Psychological Review,* 1973, *80*(6), 510–526.

SCHEIN, E. H. *Process Consultation: Its Role in Organization Development.* Reading, Mass.: Addison-Wesley, 1969.

SCHEIN, E. H., AND BENNIS, W. G. *Personal and Organizational Change Through Group Methods.* New York: Wiley, 1965.

* SCHINDLER-RAINMAN, E., AND LIPPITT, R. *Team Training for Community Change: Concepts, Goals, Strategies and Skills.* Riverside, Calif.: University of California, 1972. Description of a community change team development and action planning project. Covers diagnosis, goal setting, skill practice, action taking, feedback, and training.

* SCHMUCK, R. A., AND RUNKEL, P. J. *Organizational Training for a School Faculty.* Eugene, Ore.: CASEA, University of Oregon, 1970. Description of training and organizational development activities for a school faculty. Research results are included.

* SCHMUCK, R. A., RUNKEL, P. J., SATUREN, S., MARTELL, R., AND DERR, C. B. *Handbook of Organization Development in Schools.* Palo Alto, Calif.: National Press Books, 1973. Includes procedures for improving communications, goal setting, working with conflicts, meetings, problem solving, training designs, and evaluations. Relevant theories are presented.

SCHUTZ, W. C. *Firo: A Three-Dimensional Theory of Interpersonal Behavior.* New York: Holt, Rinehart, and Winston, 1958.

* SCHUTZ, W. C. *Joy.* New York: Grove, 1967. Many encountering exercises are presented along with discussion of their use. Main emphasis is on personal growth experiences.

SHEPARD, H. A. "Personal Growth Laboratories: Toward an Alternative Culture." *Journal of Applied Behavioral Science,* 1970, *6*(3), 259–268.

SIKES, W. W. "An Organizational Development Workshop for a College." *Social Change,* 1971, *1*(4).

SIKES, W. W., SCHLESINGER, L. E., AND SEASHORE, C. "Developing Change Agent Teams on Campus." *Journal of Higher Education,* 1973, *44*(5), 399–414.

SILBERMAN, C. E. *Crisis in the Classroom.* New York: Vintage, 1970.

SMITH, P. B. *Groups Within Organizations.* New York: Harper and Row, 1973.

SOLOMON, L. N., AND BERZON, B. (Eds.) *New Perspectives on Encounter Groups.* San Francisco: Jossey-Bass, 1972.

SPIKE, P. "Phenomenology of Today's Students." In H. L. Hodgkinson and M. B. Bloy, Jr. (Eds.), *Identity Crisis in Higher Education.* San Francisco: Jossey-Bass, 1971.

* STEVENS, J. O. *Awareness: Exploring, Experimenting, Experiencing.* Moab, Utah: Real People Press, 1971. Collection of exercises for increasing individual and group awareness. Much of the material is drawn from Gestalt psychology.

TAYLOR, H. *Students Without Teachers: The Crisis in the University.* New York: McGraw-Hill, 1969.

THELEN, H. A. *Dynamics of Groups at Work.* Chicago: University of Chicago Press, 1954.

WALTON, R. E. *Interpersonal Peacemaking: Confrontations and Third-Party Consultation.* Reading, Mass.: Addison-Wesley, 1969.

WARREN, J. R. *College Grading Practices: An Overview.* Washington, D.C.: ERIC Clearinghouse on Higher Education, 1971.

WATSON, G. "Toward a Conceptual Architecture of a Self-Renewing School System." In G. Watson (Ed.), *Change in School Systems.* Washington, D.C.: NTL, NEA, 1967.

WEISS, R., AND REIN, M. "The Evaluation of Broad Aim Programs: Difficulties in Experimental Designs and an Alternative." *Administrative Science Quarterly,* 1970, *15*(1), 97–109.

Index

A

Ability, use and expansion of, 30-33

Accreditation, team impact on, 11-12, 92-93

Action-research, concept of, 56. *See also* Change teams; Research

Administrators: ambiguous role of, 41; capabilities used by, 32

Affection in developmental process, 130

ALTER, G., 93

American Council on Education, 34

Antioch College: Washington/Baltimore as changing campus of, xii, 4, 11-12, 90-94, 105; at Yellow Springs, 21-22, 26

Applied Behavioral Science Alliance, x, xi, 4, 36, 64-70, 157. *See also* Massachusetts, University of

ARGYRIS, C., 32

ARRINGTON, L., xii, 88, 99, 100

Assessment: methods of, 162-166, 170; resources for, 165-166

Association of American Colleges, 48

AXELROD, J., 35

B

BAILIFF, L., xii, 85, 86, 101, 104-105

BARZUN, J., 20

BECKLEY, J., 87

BENEDICT, B. A., 6-7

BENNIS, W., 40

BEYTAGH, L., xii

BROOKS, G. E., 41, 42

BRUYN, S. T., 7, 8

Buffalo. *See* SUNY College at Buffalo

BUSO, M., xii

C

California, University of: grading system at Davis campus of, xii, 4, 13-14, 34-35, 84-86, 101, 104-105, 121, 123, 127, 139; at Santa Cruz, 27

Carnegie Commission on Higher Education 22, 23, 24-25, 48

Change: external factors influencing, 20-24; for group, 51; individual approaches to, 48-50; inhibitors of, 38-45; need for, 18-37; personal, 50-51; planning for, 141-143, 168-169; selecting strategy of, 95-97; value of, 39-40

Change agent, 40. *See also* Change teams

Change network. See Massachusetts, University of

Change teams: advantages of, 50-52, 57-58; appointment of, 113-115; as approach to reform, 53-63; assessment methods for, 162-166, 170; characteristics of, 1, 6, 53-54; cohesiveness of, 103-104, 106, 133-134; conceptual bases for, 1-107; conceptual model for, 2; confrontation of, 72-74; developmental activities for, 167-172; developmental models of, 6; developmental problems of, 131-137; developmental process for, 129-131; as evaluated by members, 58-60; group processes and, 135; impact of, 9-

181

16, 23-24; institutional links with, 144-147; manual for, 109-172; membership and motivation problems of, 117-119; need for, 112; needs of, 131, 170-172; objectives of, 60-61; origins of, 3-17, 112-115; outcomes for, 3-17; person-centered, 49-51; plan development by, 141-143, 168-169; power related to, 146-147; problems of, 68-70, 76-77, 79-80, 98-101; process-oriented, 140, 153-156; processes of, 9-16, 54-57, 138-143; research contribution to, 159-161; roles of members of, 146; skills of members of, 140; strategies of, 61-63; strengths of, 54; success of, 97-98; task-centered, 49-51, 72, 105; tasks for, 110. *See also* Team members

CHICKERING, A., 32

Chronicle of Higher Education, 23, 30

CINTRON, C., xii

Clients of change teams, 138-141

College and University Environment Scale, 48

Communication in team development, 131, 133

Competition as change inhibitor, 43-44

Consultant-researcher teams, 6-7

Consultants: contract setting for, 151-153; expectations of, 148-149; feedback by, 163-164; role of, 104-105, 153-156; selection of, 149-151; substitutes for, 156-158

Control in developmental process, 129-130

Council for the Advancement of Small Colleges, 48

CREAGER, J. A., 34

Creativity and higher education, 29, 32

CROSS, K. P., 23

Curricular improvement. *See* Lesley College

D

Decision-making, students involved in. *See* Utah, University of

DELONE, W., xii, 59-60

Departments: as inhibitors of change, 40-41; student advisory committee system for, 75-76

DIAZ, F., xii, 62-63

DRUCKER, P. F., 19

DUPRE, V., 65

E

EMERSON, R. W., 42

ETZIONI, A., 41, 50

F

Faculty: development programs for, 48; frustrations of, 28-37

FAIRWEATHER, G. W., 7

Feedback: by consultants, 163-164; and team development, 136-137

FELDMAN, K. A., 33

FERGUSON, M., 93

FINCH, F., xii, 59, 105

FROBES, V., 77

Fundamental Interpersonal Response Orientation (FIRO), 129-130

G

GARDNER, J. W., 42

GLEASON, R., 32

Goal Selection Matrix, 122

Goals: basis for, 121; change related to, 127-128; commitment to, 123-124, 131-132; power related to, 124-125; selection of, 121-128, 140-141, 167-168; time perspectives for, 125-127; understanding of, 122-123, 131-132

Goddard College, 26

Grading system. *See* California, University of

Group Diagnosis Matrix, 6, 172

H

HARRISON, R., 27

HAVELOCK, R. G., 43

HAYDEN, T., 20

HEFFERLIN, J. L., 20, 22, 25

HEIST, P., 29

Higher education: change needed in, 18-37; federal aid to, 21; frustrations in, 28-37; new methods and programs in, 26-28; purposes of,

24-26; responses to problems in, 45-48

HODGKINSON, H. L., 26, 35

HOWARD, K., xii, 60, 73

Human relations, technology, of, 55. *See also* SUNY College at Buffalo

I

ILLICH, I., 20

Inclusion as part of developmental process, 129

Institutional Goals Inventory, 48, 139

Issues, identification of, 168

J

JAQUES, E., 40

K

KENISTON, K., 36-37

KLEIN, D., 39

KRAUS, W., 64

L

Lesley College, improving instruction at, xii, 4, 9-10, 81-84, 98-99, 126, 139

LEWIN, K., 33, 47, 50

Life cycle, academic, as change inhibitor, 44

LIPPITT, R., 50

M

MARCHAND, L., xii

Marginality of team members, 42-43, 106-107

Massachusetts, University of: change network at, xii, 4, 14-15, 35-36, 41, 59, 64-70, 105, 126, 136, 157; Clinic to Improve University Teaching at, 48; Orchard Hill program at, 27

MEETH, R., 24

MEISLER, R., xii, 87, 99-100

Members of change teams. *See* Team members

Menninger Foundation, 130

METTY, M., 91, 92-93

MILES, M. B., 39

MILTON, O., 42

Morale of groups, 130, 169-170

N

National Institute of Mental Health (NIMH), 3, 48, 94

National Student Association, 3

National Training Laboratories (NTL), x, xi, 2, 3, 5, 22, 54, 57, 63, 65, 72, 73, 74, 75, 77-78, 80, 81, 82, 83, 84-85, 86, 88, 89, 90, 91, 93, 94, 98, 103, 105, 146, 150

New Directions students, 21

New students, 21

NEWCOMB, T. M., 33

Newman Task Force on Higher Education, 22, 48

North Central Association, 12, 93

O

Omnibus Personality Inventory, 32

Outcomes: of change teams, 3-17; for team members, 16-17

P

Parochialism as change inhibitor, 40-41

Participant-observers, 7

Participation, team development related to, 134

Policies, institutional, as change inhibitor, 43

Power: and change teams, 146-147; goals related to, 124-125

Problems: of change teams, 68-70, 76-77, 79-80, 98-101; overcoming, 101-105; responses to, 45-47

Problem-solving as change team approach, 71-72

Process, concept of, 56

Puerto Rico, University of, relevance of psychology program at, xii, 4, 10, 26, 62-63, 72, 73, 74, 78-81, 114, 135, 139, 140

Purdue Rating Scale for Instructors, 83-84

Pyramidal values, 32-33

R

Racism in higher education, 23-24

RAFFERTY, M., 20

RASKIN, M., 50

Rebellion as individual approach to change, 49

REICHENTHAL, C., 88

REID, T., 85

REIN, M., 9

Relevance in psychology department. *See* Puerto Rico, University of

Research: action-oriented, 159-166; assessment methods in, 162-166; contribution of, to team, 159-161; goals of, 161-162

Researcher-documentarian, role of, 5-6

Resource Committee on Student Participation. *See* Utah, University of

Rewards and team development, 134-135

RICHARDS, V., 84

Rockefeller Foundation, 21

RODRIGUEZ, I., xii

ROGERS, C., 27-28

ROURKE, F. E., 41, 42

S

SARASON, S. B., 110

SASHKIN, M., 6

SCHLESINGER, L. E., x, xi

SCHUTZ, W. C., 129-130

SEASHORE, C., xi, 3

Self-direction, concept of, 52

Settings, creating new, 110

Sexism in higher education, 23-24

SHOFFEITT, P., xii, 93, 94, 105

SIKES, W. W., x, xi, 78, 84

Skills, lack of change-oriented, 42

SLATTERY, J., xii, 98-99

SPIKE, P., 35

State University of New York. *See* SUNY at Old Westbury; SUNY College at Buffalo

Strategies for Change and Knowledge Utilization, 48

Student Affairs Team. *See* Virgin Islands, College of the

Student services. *See* Virgin Islands, College of the

Students: decision-making by, *see* Utah, University of; disadvantaged, at Antioch, 21; frustrations of, 28-37; stress reduction for, 3; values of, 23

SUNDERLAND, S., xi, 3

SUNY at Old Westbury, 26

SUNY College at Buffalo, human relations services at, xii, 4, 12-13, 27, 86-90, 99-100, 136

T

TAYLOR, H., 25

Team members: in consultant role, 156-157; evaluations by, 58-60; feelings of, 168; growth experiences for, 170; loyalty between, 133-134; marginal positions of, 42-43, 106-107; motivations of, 116-117; objectives of, 60; outcomes for, 16-17; recruitment of, 116-120; skill development in, 131-132; turnover among, 102

Teams. *See* Change teams

THOMAS, W. F., xii, 71, 73-74, 75

U

Union for Experimenting Colleges and Universities, 48

Unions in higher education, 24

Utah, University of, decision-making by students at, xii, 4, 10-11, 63, 75-78, 114-115, 127, 135, 147

V

Values: among new programs, 27; pyramidal, 32-33; shifts in, 23; of teams and institution, 147

VINCENT, H., xii, 63

Virgin Islands, College of the (CVI), student services at, xii, 4, 15-16, 59-60, 70-75, 113, 125, 127

Volunteers, maintenance of, as change inhibitor, 44-45

W

WATSON, G., 50

WEISS, R., 9

Withdrawal as individual approach to change, 49

WOERNER, S., 86

Workshops: assessment of, 163-164; as substitute for consultants, 157-158

Wright Institute, 48